Confessions of a Circuit Rider

Confessions of a Circuit Rider

A Marginal Chaplain's Apocalyptic and Disjointed Journal

STEPHEN FALLER

CASCADE *Books* • Eugene, Oregon

CONFESSIONS OF A CIRCUIT RIDER
A Marginal Chaplain's Apocalyptic and Disjointed Journal

Copyright © 2023 Stephen Faller. All rights reserved. Except for brief quotations in critical publications or reviews, no part of this book may be reproduced in any manner without prior written permission from the publisher. Write: Permissions, Wipf and Stock Publishers, 199 W. 8th Ave., Suite 3, Eugene, OR 97401.

Cascade Books
An Imprint of Wipf and Stock Publishers
199 W. 8th Ave., Suite 3
Eugene, OR 97401

www.wipfandstock.com

PAPERBACK ISBN: 978-1-6667-7030-8
HARDCOVER ISBN: 978-1-6667-7031-5
EBOOK ISBN: 978-1-6667-7032-2

Cataloguing-in-Publication data:

Names: Faller, Stephen, author.

Title: Confessions of a circuit rider : a marginal chaplain's apocalyptic and disjointed journal / Stephen Faller.

Description: Eugene, OR: Cascade Books, 2023. | Includes bibliographical references.

Identifiers: ISBN 978-1-6667-7030-8 (paperback) | ISBN 978-1-6667-7031-5 (hardcover) | ISBN 978-1-6667-7032-2 (ebook)

Subjects: LCSH: Pastoral care. | Pastoral theology. | Spiritual direction.

Classification: BV4011.3 F36 2023 (paperback) | BV4011 (ebook)

12/21/23

Contents

Chapter 1	The Secret	1
Chapter 2	The Lie	11
Chapter 3	The Circuit Rider	21
Chapter 4	The Margins	26
Chapter 5	The Exodus	33
Chapter 6	The Traveler's Cloak	38
Chapter 7	The Adoption	43
Chapter 8	The Good, the Bad, and the Ugly	49
Chapter 9	The Letters	59
Chapter 10	The Chasm	67
Chapter 11	The Fairy Tale	84
Chapter 12	The Name	92
Chapter 13	The Harrowing	97
Chapter 14	The Road	106
Chapter 15	The Individual	112
Chapter 16	The Midwife	119
Chapter 17	The Question	131
Chapter 18	The Fire	134
Chapter 19	The Desert	143
Chapter 20	The Apocalypse	151
Recommended Reading		161
Recommended Music		163

CHAPTER 1

The Secret

In any weather, at any hour of the day or night,
I have been anxious to improve the nick of time,
and notch it on my stick too;
to stand on the meeting of two eternities, the past and future,
which is precisely the present moment;
to toe that line.
You will pardon some obscurities,
for there are more secrets in my trade than in most men's,
and yet not voluntarily kept, but inseparable from its very nature.
I would gladly tell all that I know about it,
and never paint "No Admittance" on my gate.

THOREAU

The Collect for Purity
Almighty God,
unto whom all hearts are open,
all desires known,
and from whom no secrets are hid;
cleanse the thoughts of our hearts by the inspiration of thy Holy Ghost,
that we may perfectly love thee,
and worthily magnify thy Holy Name;
through Christ our Lord.
Amen.

1

All secrets are mine.

I am in the business of secrets. Much of what happens between a patient and a chaplain is a secret.

When I say "all secrets are mine," I mean many things. I am a collector of secrets, and each is my responsibility. It is mine to welcome them and hold them. I am their keeper; their ward. They are my charge. I mean these things, and more.

One welcomes a secret like catching a child; boiling water and rending sheets.

And it's a birthday.

All don't survive.

Of course that might seem like hyperbole, which is probably the only thing I can speak fluently. But, be assured, I have traveled these roads—these and some unfit for print. Our second child is buried in Titusville. Like the smaller table at Thanksgiving, there is a section in the back of the cemetery reserved for children. These things don't start off as secrets, but only my wife and children will accept the invitation to Titusville, the rest of the family declines.

All secrets are mine, and I will start with the one that has never been a secret, except for here, which is that I have a physical disability and I use a wheelchair. Everyone else can see it; there's no cat in this bag. My name is Chaplain Stephen Faller. I will share myself with you. We will probably disagree; that's the point, right? I have learned about the interweaving of joy and sorrow. From my life and my chaplaincy, I have learned that the most poignant births are for those who have one date on their stone; birth and death are one. But I will also share what I have learned about love, which is a way of expressing love to you, and I mean it. I will not judge you; my inquiry is pointed elsewhere.

I mean many things.

2

Sometimes things become secretive because of the difficulty in transmission. Things that are not inherently secretive become very private over time because they are nearly impossible to share. Chaplaincy carries many of these characteristics. But I am this chaplain, and this is a trivial profession (referring to the *via triviales*) that is known by very few. I will share with you what this is, and who I am, but it is complex and it is not easily told. Secrets are compounded by lies, which make any kind of truthtelling extremely difficult.

What is a chaplain? It depends how you answer. Really. The answering of the question is what defines the chaplain. Some people will say, "A chaplain is an interfaith member of the healthcare team that ensures holistic treatment through spiritual care."

This chaplain would not. Chaplaincy is a type of ministry where the clergy operates beyond the four walls of institutional ministry. That is, beyond the church building, beyond the synagogue, beyond the temple. If that is true, then what defines the chaplaincy is its location outside. Therefore, it's a conceptual error to define it inside somewhere else, specifically, by whatever random setting where it happens. There are chaplains in healthcare, schools and colleges, prisons, hospice, police and fire, military, nursing homes, disasters, psychiatric, and really anything you can think of. There are trucker chaplains and mariner chaplains.

It's also important that what defines a chaplain is not being "an interfaith member," but rather, that the chaplain is clergy. I mean no disrespect to those who are ordained interfaith, among whom I'm met several sacred souls. Of course in a pluralistic society, if a clergy has no interfaith skills, they are going to quickly burn more bridges than they build and that leads to a short chaplaincy, but sometimes being interfaith can be confused with a lack of identity. Chaplains have identity.

In the hurry of things, and the rush to communicate things quickly, the lust for being recognized rather than understood, chaplains can say things very quickly for the sake of expediency. It is hard to explain that I'm a particular believer that has the particular calling of serving anyone. The shorthand is: we are interfaith. I am not. It is even more expedient for chaplains to let others define them. Tragic, then, that the meaning of chaplaincy lies in how you answer.

There is a fine line between saying "every religion is the same" and "no religion is true." I will be concerned about fine lines—even obsessed with them. Because what makes any path valid is its intimacy with God. What is disclosed in the Bible is the revelation of a particular God. If the conversation about religion loses all particularity, it also loses all holiness. Inclusivity easily becomes exclusivity. Religion without holiness becomes magic and its relics may become magic items. God likes to whisper so closely you can feel the breath. Revealing and committing. Intimacy.

God has touched me in a personal way. I cannot list all of the ways God has ever acted, or might ever act. I can begin to explore how God has acted with me. Convicted by that experience, my chaplaincy is about helping other people reach toward God in a personal way—even if I cannot understand it. The alternative would be to put my own understanding first, and I try not to lean on that. So, because of how much my own personal religion has meant to me, I think the best thing I can do for another is to help their own personal religion, which by definition I cannot understand.

My own chaplaincy started in long-term care facilities. That was in Durham, and I'm still amazed to have supported those who had known and loved veterans of the Civil War. My chaplaincy then took me to a community hospital, a homeless shelter, and then the Durham VA, all in Carolina. Then I came to New Jersey, where I trained at Trenton Psych, Albert Einstein in Philadelphia, and then I landed at a small two-hospital system in Trenton. Later, when my second child was born, I picked up a part-time job at a psych hospital, Carrier Clinic. By this time I had started teaching chaplaincy, and I had students in nursing homes and a nearby hospice. All of these contexts have informed my theology of chaplaincy, and then some.

Something happens in the telling of the secret, thus much of the currency is in catharsis. And I would say that practically speaking, little of the work happens through formal absolution and reconciliation. By far, most of the power is around secret bearing.

Bearing as in the secret is a burden. Because the greatest confession is a life that has never been understood by anyone. Each year, it gets heavier. How are we to pass through life's gate without being understood? The secret is a heavy thing on a long journey, and there is so much that has never been spoken because no one could ever have the time to hear it.

Bearing as in the secret must be born and birthed. Birthing is always about secret. Birthing is about the breaking open of the secret, about bringing something forth that has been impossible and unimaginable.

Perhaps these are not different meanings. Perhaps these are the same words and the same meaning. Perhaps bearing a secret is so spiritually heavy that you feel like you are being pulled apart from within as if you were giving birth. It is time to tell some secrets.

You might want the children in the other room.

There is and there is no Santa Claus. That is: there is; and, there is no, Santa Claus.

The movie *Miracle on 34th Street* argues that yes, there is a Santa Claus. There are very tangible ways that this very fictional character has touched many people. Yes, there's the emotional sentiment that people have, but the material merchandising is astronomical. There are enough plastic Santas to reach from here to the moon. There are enough patriarchs in Santa cosplay every year to make an army.

There is an Orthodox Saint Nicholas who lived a real life who is a real saint. A real saint who served poor children and was imprisoned. He was a bishop. He was even at the Council of Nicea.

It is also true that in the 1930s, infernal Coca-Cola developed a high-powered advertising campaign to link a certain red can with a certain red suit. The artist hailed from Morristown, New Jersey, and I regard the art as some of the most iconic pop art I've ever seen. It's not Norman Rockwell, but I love the art and it immediately evokes the season. It is worth noting that Santa Claus was not connected with American merchandising before this campaign.

It is also amazing how many links there are between the Santa Claus tradition and pagan religions and the winter solstice. Down to the flying reindeer.

There is and there is no Santa Claus. This is a secret which is also a pointer to a deeper secret. Dear Heraclitus knew this secret, and published it to the world. He said, "It is and is not the same thing." With our cultural clichés, it has been chic to say, "That's a thing," and, "It is what it is," and I did my best to buck these vile clichés for the sake of Heraclitus and free thought everywhere. (I have also been guilty of inserting, "I don't know, wrong?" in place of, "I know, right?"—language itself being a dialectic between creativity and conformity.)

The power of this secret is subversive. There are many, many things that are and are not true at the same time. This goes against Aristotelian thought and philosophy's "Law of the Excluded Middle." This is radical. Completely true and completely untrue. In a binary existence, reality is quantum. This secret exposes the great failure of deconstructionism. The power of Derrida has been that we are saturated with meaning, utterly drenched with it. A text, therefore, cannot have one and only one meaning. The perversion of deconstruction by the academy has been that the text has no meaning at all. The brilliance of Heraclitus is a lot more in alignment with Derrida. This gets a theological gloss when he says, "G-d does, and yet does not, consent to be called Zeus." This reverence of the Divine Name here inspires me to hide the vowel, because we so clearly have not been given the Divine Name. And to Heraclitus's point, we seem to be perfectly happy calling the Almighty whatever we want and for some reason the Almighty permits this.

It is worth a second look. Things are and are not the same thing. We are and are not Americans. We are and are not Germans. We are and are not faithful. We are and we are not religious. America is and is not racist. It is and is not sexist. There are and there are not two Americas. I could really draw this out. There was and was not an insurrection. It was and was not on January 6. There is and there is not a White America. There is and there is not a Black America. America is and is not an empire. Insofar as there are two Americas, with completely opposing value systems, they are occupying the exact same space and time. Same longitude same latitude.

3

The reader may be hoping for an example, or a "case study." That is, they may be hoping for a revelation, where slowly and carefully a secret has been shared with me, and then in turn I might share this with the reader. That I would show you someone showing me. That in my description I might share a meta-secret; that I might share the secret of soliciting the secret. I know this because I have been guilty of the same desire, and this itself might be the only meta-secret that there is. And by the way, that would only make me the worst confessor ever, to spend a lifetime collecting secrets of the holy and unholy, and then to share them with whatever poor soul willing to read this book. No one escapes irony: not me, and not you.

But this meta-secret is true. There is only a false dichotomy between us and them, all are one, subject transubstantiates into object, confessor and penitent are the same. In my own lust for knowledge, I have scoured the biographies of St. John Vianney, the patron saint of confession itself, only to find absolutely nothing useful. One finds only a beatified veneration of a priest for whom sinners would queue for miles on bloody knees, but not one clinical depiction of how he took the confession.

In addition to the secrets I have collected, I have generated secrets of my own. These vary in nature; some trivially personal, some tragic. There are many dialectics to describe them. Some of them are the things that the fewest people know about me—things I don't want anyone to know. And there are some that I would like everyone to know.

In my heart, I have really only ever written one book, including this one. Some of the books are published, some unpublished. Some are articles online that might still be found, some chapters in other books. They are all about taking up the journey away from dualism.

There was one book I wrote that might truly seem "off-topic." This was the book *Reality TV*. There are two versions of this book, and the first is completely lost. It had a more philosophical and theoretical feel, and it explored the world of illusion and simulacra against the world of reality. The book that got published was essentially a discussion guide for adult groups. There is some brilliance of the former book that survived into the latter in an image of communion.

The image was a little complicated so I'll try to describe it here. I prefer "communion" to the Greek "eucharist" because communion is a multivalent word and I prefer words with more meaning. "Communion" describes the assemblage of the body of Christ; namely, the believers who have gathered. But immediately, it also aspires to the Divine Communion, the transcendence through which we commune with the Godhead. All of this has a hopeful expectation of the "communion of saints" which connects me to those who partook in the rite yesterday, and those who will partake tomorrow.

But there is also something spelled out in the logistics, the sheer mechanics, of the rite. This is the choreography of the liturgical dance. In such pageantry the penitent themselves become the symbol of veneration. It is a moving symbol and a symbol of motion across time. They take up postures and poses that are more profound than all of the stained glass that surrounds them. How do you get bread and wine (taking in both kinds) to all those people? What emerges is a beautiful embodiment of the relationship between the individual and the group. Because it's both. There is none of this "communion of saints" for one person, alone. And this is why the sacrament shall never be single, self-serve. Communion that is shared with the sick has been consecrated at the Mass for all (as the word suggests).

But what is said to the individual? What are the words of institution? "The blood of Christ, poured out for you." "The blood of Christ, shed for you." These words are just as important as the that the elements are consecrated in collective worship. In these words the individual is elevated to the attention of the Almighty. For one, relatively insignificant, person the blood of Christ has been shed. That's exquisitely important and it should never be erased by the academic heresy that the blood of Christ is only poured out for the bulk, no for the entire cosmos, diffused throughout infinity itself. No, with those words the incarnation takes a focused concentration again. And for a brief second, All has been sacrificed for one. It is a perfect manifestation of the essential dialectic between the individual and the group. Otherwise the individual only exists to be consumed by the group, the communicants become cannibals, and Love itself is annihilated.

It should also be noted that the tension between the world of reality and the world of simulacra is both the means and ends of dualism, but this is getting ahead of things.

I don't know if anyone has read all my published books at all, and then if they have realized that it is one book. But it is. This is not because of a master design. I'm just stuck on the same page. When I teach chaplaincy, I require that the students ask themselves to examine what has not been heard. The easiest way to see what has not been heard, often precisely because the chaplain refuses to hear it, is that which the patient repeats. They keep trying, over and over again, to express themselves. Like me.

My first published book was *Beyond the Matrix*. This book was about the pop culture movies of the same name that appeared in the year 2003, published 2004. Those movies still exert a strange influence to this day: the Far Right call themselves "red pills," while the Far Left call themselves "woke." And that is a book about many things. It is about Plato's Cave, and the prison of appearances and finding the freedom of reality. It is about the prison of dualism, and our experience of it. It has only ever been one book. It has only been the struggle to be free and to help others get there.

My other two books were about the same thing. The timeline gets a little trippy in the retrospective, because although they are the most recently published, they were written much earlier. My work on spiritual midwifery was written in 2000, and that was based on an academic journey spanning from 1992 to 1999. That book tries to help restore spiritual movement, often when mired in psychoreligious dualisms. My other work explores my own journey toward chaplaincy, with much thought given to the dualisms that have shaped our culture since 9/11. I will say more about this book later. This is my secret that I most want to share, literally what I have published to the world. "Welcome," painted on my gate.

I was hoping that I was going to have it all figured out by the time I started writing this book. That sounds ridiculous, but I was honestly hoping to present the reader a few more polished concepts and ideas that were more complete. I approached the project with questions and I wanted to return with answers. It's been ten years since I have written anything of this scope. I am reminded of Pascal: "When I consider the short duration of my life, swallowed up in the eternity before and after, and the little space I fill, and even can see, engulfed in the infinite immensity of space of which I am ignorant, and which knows me not, I am frightened, and am astonished at being here rather than there, why now rather than then." That's from his collection of thoughts, the *Pensées*. I am deeply delighted by the dialectical construction of this expression. It resonates through my entire being. I am stupefied by my own stupidity. I am humbled. I am frightened. Perhaps I am like Job. I was not there. I did not tumble with Leviathan. I am like Jonah. I am swallowed.

Before I convince the reader that buying this book was a mistake, I am confessing my secret of where this book is coming from. I am having to write this book not knowing, without all the answers. My understanding is an unfinished project. I'm at a place now where the only conclusion is that there is no conclusion. Not for me. The journey is endless. Waiting for all the answers before writing is a vow to not write. I do not know.

But I am ready.

4

Catching a secret.

There are trade secrets of this secretive trade. Yes, there are little tricks and gimmicks that accelerate the work. There are inducives that quicken and stimulate the midwifery that this is. There are plenty of stupid things that one can do which interfere and interrupt this sacred work. Pray and prepare. Be patient and expect to be challenged and tested. Don't ask too many questions. Don't make it about you.

But there are three much bigger secrets here, which I will quickly name. The first is that you have to want the secret with every fiber of your being. This is harder than it sounds. Like a child untimely born, no secret can be too ugly for the chaplain to catch. When the patient begins to share that which is ugly, begin to desire that which is uglier. When the patient begins to share that which is dark, start to desire that which is darker. What may be lost on the reader is the obvious horror. Why do I have to even say this in the first place? Why is it even necessary to exhort the chaplain in something more fundamental than the most strident fundamentalist? Because chaplains don't naturally want dark and ugly secrets. And yes, it is the case that some of the presentations are absolutely hideous, but in truth the most frightening thing of all is that once the secret is out in all of its living and writhing glory, the chaplain remains a person *who does not know how to respond and this is terrifying*. As long as the secret does not come out this is not a problem. As long as we trade in pleasantries and saccharine kindness, no one is worse for the wear and the underlying ignorance (truly that which is ignored) can remain hidden. Looks like two secrets, doesn't it? The baby and the bastard, but the bastard belongs to the chaplain.

The second secret is that the secret is a secret even unto the one who bears the secret. You read that right: the person telling the secret does not know what it means. They only know that it is extremely intense, and should push come to shove, they will describe that intensity as painful. As the secret crests like a river and crowns like a baby it is quite likely that the birthgiver has all kinds of confused ideas about what this means, what it has meant, and what it will come to mean. They will naturally believe that the meaning of the secret is found within the ineffable intensity. But that's not so. This experience, whatever it was, was so intense that it has likely changed how they know God. And that's a problem. Because God is the source of all meaning. So the important thing is not that something really intense happened on some Monday, but rather that this really intense thing categorically changed their understanding of God and possibly disrupted their connection to the source of all meaning.

The third secret is that this is the most important work in the world. I'll say it again: this is the most important work ever. I have met so many patients that promise to write a book. They have not. They will not. Let's dispense with the pretense. There is no forthcoming memoir. And yet, there is a story that must be told. The fate of the universe depends on it, and the only pages where it will be written is their holy dialogue with God (and you).

I can't say that I've seen it all, but I've seen a lot. "Seeing" isn't quite the right word because this approaches the categories of hope and faith, which rely on things that are unseen. Secrets are "heard." No two days of this ministry have been the same; there is always something new and unimaginable. It is constant amazement. I have met many people.

I have met someone . . . who found and lost their entire family of multiple generations on the same day—even in the same moment. Who lost a child, and someone else who has just conceived. Someone who has wanted a baby, and someone who has wanted the baby gone. Someone whose child was abducted. Someone who has lost a home. Who has lost a father. Who has lost a mother. Lost grandparents. Someone who has won 100,000 dollars and someone who has declared bankruptcy. Who has lost a car. Someone who has lived in a car. Another who was not so lucky to live in a car but to sleep on a bathroom floor. Who has lost employment. Who has moved into a home only for the dryer to catch fire a week later. Car accidents of every degree. Who has been traumatically injured and someone who has been traumatized. Who has psychiatric issues. Anxiety disorder, depression, you name it. Who has been abused. Bullied. Who has been betrayed, left for dead. Who has been mugged. Good marriages, bad marriages, and bed bugs. Broken bones. Broken homes. I suppose if you put all these people together, they would be Job.

All secrets are mine.

CHAPTER 2

The Lie

Then said Jesus to those Jews which believed on him,
If ye continue in my word, then are ye my disciples indeed;
And ye shall know the truth, and the truth shall make you free.
They answered him, We be Abraham's seed,
and were never in bondage to any man:
how sayest thou, Ye shall be made free?
Jesus said unto them, If God were your Father, ye would love me:
for I proceeded forth and came from God; neither came I of myself,
but he sent me. Why do ye not understand my speech?
even because ye cannot hear my word.
Ye are of your father the devil, and the lusts of your father ye will do.
He was a murderer from the beginning, and abode not in the truth,
because there is no truth in him.
When he speaketh a lie, he speaketh of his own:
for he is a liar, and the father of it.
And because I tell you the truth, ye believe me not.
THE GOSPEL ACCORDING TO JOHN

5

Riddle me this. A person comes to a fork in the road, a fork with two doors, and two guardians thus. In unison say they, "Welcome traveler. Your journey has brought you this far, and on this accomplishment congratulations are due. Your journey is about to achieve salvation or damnation, and we know not which. Permitted are you one question, and only one question are you permitted. For one door will bring you eternal bliss and the other door will bring you eternal torment. We guardians have been sent to help you find your path. You may direct your question to me or my brother, but my brother always lies (they both accuse the other: one, in truth; the other, in deceit). But rest assured, because I always tell the truth. My word is my bond."

This is the best riddle ever. I'll discuss the riddle, and then answer the riddle. The daring reader is recommended to pause here and wrestle as long as you like, even like Israel, until the morning comes. You get one question, and from this answer you may ferret where freedom lies. There is no trick answer, like waiting for someone else to come along—there is no other way out of the paradoxical paradigm. It is a logic puzzle, akin to the best that were shared on the radio show *Car Talk*. Just to pick at it for a minute, you can ask a question to one of the guardians about which you know the truth and through which you can figure out who is the liar and who is the truthteller. But then you've used up your question. You have to figure out who has the truth, and which door to take, and you only get one.

Good luck.

Spiritually speaking, that category of "truthteller" is very important. Before there was philosophy and philosophers, people were servants of *Aletheia*, that is, people who told the truth. I like to think that my namesake, Stephen the Martyr, was a throwback to this older tradition, because once the truth is out there it changes things. *Lethe* is the river of forgetting that one must cross in the underworld. The things that you don't forget, the things that you must remember, are truth.

One can research this riddle. One can research anything these days. On the internet, this is known as the "Knights and Knaves" riddle. This riddle was popularized by Raymond Smullyan's book in the late 1970s, and was preceded by an episode of *Doctor Who* in 1975. I would see this years later in the 1980s. It's a peculiar genealogy with roots to the 1950s, and the apparent need to locate the riddle within human thought to me is as curious as the riddle itself. The riddle has appeared in two additional pieces of pop culture sci-fi and fantasy, all three of which have found their way to my eyes. Each roughly a decade apart. And it appears here.

The riddle makes more obvious sense if you borrow a little from mathematics. If one guardian grants a positive answer, and the other a negative answer, then the problem is that you don't know which is which. You don't know which you've got hold of. But, if you could cross them—*entangle* them—then you know you've got a negative answer. Like multiplying a positive number against a negative one. If you knew you were getting a lie, you could just do the opposite and you'd have the truth. Binaries are nice that way. So the magic question to be asked is, "If I were to ask your brother, which door would he say?" No matter which you speak to, if both brothers play their role faithfully, you will get a lie. If you are addressing the liar, that's a sure lie, and the truthteller will report, accurately, that the liar will answer with a lie.

This . . . is . . . the human condition. This is the predicament that every single person finds themselves in. This little riddle is a parable of life itself. I say parable, because this is exactly the rhetorical logic that Jesus uses all the time. Yes, I mean logic. Any time he starts up, "A man had two sons . . ." this is exactly where he's headed. Like the riddle about the lies, the parable crosses the logic where the good son does the bad thing and the bad son does the good thing. And what do we find in the entangled logic? *Ourselves.* This is the human condition. We do not know. This very veil of not-knowing hides the birth of faith.

I want to say something more about not knowing. It is comfortable to have a materialistic view of the universe, because it creates the impression that we know what things are and what they mean. Life has a clear beginning and a clear end—the one who can understand them both, as well as everything in between, can breathe easy. And it also establishes humanity as the smartest thing in the universe, which is very arrogant. The materialist denies this, and says, "I have to be brave and confront death."

It is comfortable to have a Christian fundamentalist view of the universe, and to think that the universe is ten thousand years old. This person believes that the world was created so that its mountains appear millions of years old, staged that way. It creates a similar context of knowing everything that is important. The fundamentalist denies this and says, "I have to be brave and face God about my sins and make sure my thoughts are right."

The secret is that it is uncomfortable to not know.

6

We need to talk about lies.

Chaplaincy doesn't interest itself with lies. It is not the business of lying, or decoding the lies one has been told.

It is not the business of lying, although there have been times I have been asked to withhold information from families. I find this posture very uncomfortable, and have grown significant distaste for prying into medical charts before I meet people. I do not like to dissimulate. Of course, there are reasons for this. I'm not medical and people always have medical questions, but yeah, if I've been asked to show up it's probably not a good day for somebody. In these spaces, I get very lawyerly. "I do not know all that has happened with your loved one, but someone will be here to answer both of our questions very soon." I had to say that as a chaplain resident, and the patient was dead.

Nor is chaplaincy the business of decoding lies, and especially not trying to catch people in them. I will be the first to admit it, I can be fooled. I had one patient who claimed to be one of the sacred Kohenim, and he was actually a very controversial and questionable sex author. Although, in his own way, he was a beautiful person, and I'm glad to have taken the time to care about him. It is, however, extremely important to develop the ability to hear between the lines, even between the lines of spoken speech, to hear what people are really saying. The reason for this is that the truth is so hard to tell for people. And they lie to themselves. Often.

So, why do lies matter? Two reasons. If there is healing in bearing secrets and telling the truth, lies just ruin all that. They damage the soul.

The other reason is that one day someone is going to ask the chaplain, "Is there any reason to have hope?" And you don't want to be a stranger to truth in that moment. You don't want this time to be the first moment you have thought about the answer.

You cannot spend enough time with Genesis. The whole tradition is built on that text. Every chapter lays foundations. Every chapter, every verse, every space between verses. And we think we know exactly what it says, and exactly what it means. In chapter 3, we find the first lie. We might be tempted to skip over it without a thought, as if it were a fairy tale that has become boring. God has created by speaking, and the serpent destroys by lying. I'm going to highlight two things that you probably somewhat recognize already.

One more preamble. Just go with me—however you read the text. If you think it's myth, or if you think it's history, or anywhere in between. No matter what you think about the text, it's in the front of the Book for a reason. Although that reason may not be what you think it was.

The first thing, then, is the lie itself. In chapter 3, verses 4 and 5, "And the serpent said unto the woman, Ye shall not surely die: For God doth know that in the day ye eat thereof, then your eyes shall be opened, and ye shall be as gods, knowing good and evil." The sin happens forthwith right in the next verse. There's a little bit between the lines there that is not there explicitly, and it is a key part of the process. Because between every idea and every action is the belief that this is going to end well. Nobody sets out to ruin their own life. But we all set out, and set out to bend the rules, because we think it is going to get us somewhere good.

The alternative is even more unthinkable. Let's say Eve knows full well that this is going to end badly. Then what? Then she has to think that she can get away with it. The text almost suggests this as Adam and Eve think they can actually succeed with hiding. "Whither can thou goest to get away from Thee?" one has to ask. It is like the little girl who hides from the monster under her bedsheet. If she cannot see the monster, the monster cannot see her. But this is just not how it works, little girl, and however hard we strive to blot God out of our own vision, God has no problem finding us right where we live.

But this does introduce a problem of its own: the problem of counter-will. Paul will talk about this centuries later when he talks about not being able to do the things he wants to, but doing the things he does not. This is all counter-will. For him, the catalyst is the Law itself, but Eve demonstrates that the Law need not be more complicated than a single tree in the garden. In the struggle for individuation, the path for autonomy only appears like rebellion. The only way to be oneself is to rebel. This is a real problem, which the Bible doesn't name at all, save for Paul. The most basic theological assertion of the whole book is that there is a Divine Creator. Eve reveals the burden of being creation. What do we utter in this Divine Dialogue if all the "Good" words have been taken? God gets all the good lines. God says, "Let there be," and it's all good. Except it's not. How are we to find ourselves? If Thine is the glory, what's left for me? The serpent, it seems, knows this too well, and uses this aspect of human nature for the torque of his temptation. If we start off, and you tell me what to do, my choices are to be a slave or rebel.

Even a good idea looks bad. There was a physicist joke in the 1990s playing off of a seat belt promotion campaign. The bumper sticker read, "Gravity: It's Not Just a Good Idea, It's the Law." The joke is: imagine life without gravity, which gets really silly, really fast. But even the law of gravity feels oppressive through the lens of counter-will. And every parent knows this. "Honey, please don't stick that in your nose," practically becomes a mandate to plug every nostril. That is, every parent except God? But somehow it happens. Somehow we all discover that we do not know more than our parents, and we become free to live our lives without foreign objects lodged in our faces. And Paul expresses the terrifying hope, that we can submit to God and be ourselves, that we can find ourselves in God and be embraced but not consumed. This is all that Paul ever meant when he tries to talk about submission before God.

Notice that all of this is between the lines. Literally between verses 5 and 6.

The final point here is the serpent's lie. Does it look strange? That's because it's not a lie. *The serpent doesn't lie.* The serpent deceives with the truth here. It says, "surely you won't die," and surely they don't. Banished though they may be, they sure enough walk right out of there on their own two legs. This is not like my parable riddle, such that the serpent has to robotically lie under the programming. Deceit is much more convincing when truth is used as the deception. So the serpent speaks truth, and it is a truth that deceives. Completely corrupt. Completely horrifying.

The next piece is about the Tree. I have dreamed of this Tree. This is not the Tree of Knowledge of Good and Evil, that's got to be a misnomer. This is the Tree of Dualism. Has it occurred to you that the Tree of Knowledge of Good would have been enough? If I dedicate my life to understanding that which is good, and everything about God is good, and everything God does is good, isn't that good enough? Do I really need to throw in evil?

The reader doesn't notice it. In Genesis 1, God has already created the great antinomies: light and dark, day and night, water and dry, male and female—in just a few words, engenderment and sexuality are as firmly established as the celestial firmament. Many of these things are just consequential to existence. If you have a body, and light, you're going to have shadow. So, what's one more antinomy, right? Good and evil, right? Except that the Tree is one container that holds these opposites, and thus the Tree of Dualism. Let me say it a little more strongly: when the Tree of Knowledge is introduced right after the great antinomies of being, we just take it in as one more. We don't look at it. We don't question it. It's not even the "Tree of Knowledge from 'A' to 'Z' from Alpha to Omega," but specifically good and that which is not. Bunched in the basket with the rest of reality we hardly notice the Tree of Dualism.

It is worth noting that no other story about the garden of Eden has two trees. Every other such story has the Tree of Life, which also appears in Genesis. Not the Akkadian or Babylonian accounts before, nor the Islamic accounts thereafter have this Tree of Dualism. The latter is especially fascinating because the Quran has so much of the same, and I suspect it is Islam's underlying Persian consciousness that lends to the omission, because the Persian consciousness seems to have preceded Hebrew authorship.

Why does the Tree of Dualism appear in the Hebrew Bible only? It is a good question, and every possibility is a good answer. Of course the very fact that it appears at all is telling. This Tree of Opposing Contrasts lends itself to be opposed and contrasted to the Tree of Life. Insinuating what? That the opposite of Life is Dualism.

I would be remiss to not say that there were sociopolitical factors at the time Genesis was written, that would have made it very appealing for the story to have an overarching frame of Dualism. This was the time of Cyrus, who was very committed to effecting a state religion of Zoroastrianism, and it is very coincidental that Dualism makes people easier to control. Dualism is the mythological hook that is baited and barbed (double barbed). We swallow it because we are hungry and starving. But it is metal and it is poison and it cannot come out without killing you.

What if Dualism itself *is* the fall? That is, what if every time someone entered into a mindset where Good is over here and Evil is over there, the fall happens? Maybe the fall is an ongoing problem. Because once we see things that way, we imagine ourselves on the side of the Good and everyone we disagree with on the side of Evil. Maybe the fall is when we convince ourselves that we can go through life without God—that I am having this experience and God is not a part of it. This is as far as you can get from Psalm 139, "If I ascend up into heaven, thou art there: if I make my bed in hell, behold, thou art there." Truly as far as the east is from the west.

This seems evident in the curses of Adam. What do people do in this life? They have to toil. They do something to get the food into their mouths. It's not like there was DoorDash before the fall. What was Adam doing before? Keeping the garden—that is, labor. What was he doing after? Labor. What changed? Perspective, communion, and a curse. Without God, our very predicament becomes a curse.

7

You can say a lot of things about gas that costs $3.99. You can say it's highway robbery. You can also put so much pressure on me and squeeze me so hard that I will say it's a good deal. You can say that it's the work of the evil corporation stealing from the worker. You can say it's a political trick. You can even say that it's $4.00.

I think that what it is, is something much worse. My children were mortified when I told them about the fractional penny. There is no such thing as gas that's $3.99. It's $3.99 and 9/10 of a penny. The actual price is $3.999. I don't know how you manage to split the penny. Like the plot of *Superman III* or a bad joke, we end up paying 9/10 of a cent and don't even know it.

But what is 1/1000th of a dollar worth? Apparently, the truth. People will lie for as little as 1/1000th of a dollar. And these lies are proclaimed on every corner and no one blushes. It is a lie, and the whole purpose of the lie is so you don't look past the first digit. This is exactly how the entire culture is built. This is how the priests and prophets of fake news can in themselves both be fake. Moreover, it is the lie we accept. We know that the actual cost is $3.999 and we know that this is done to make it look less than $4.000. We know that this effort is made because something that starts with three looks smaller than something with four. We know that this is done to shape human behavior. And . . . it's fine.

My assertion is that this liar riddle is the human condition.

What happens in every movie that begins with someone telling the hero, "Trust no one"? Who do you think is going to be revealed as the villain?

When Bill Clinton says, "Yes, I did lie," does that make him more believable? Why? It shouldn't. There's a little gimmick here with inductive logic. I use this riddle as a set piece when I'm teaching inductive logic. Irony primes the pump of inductive logic, and its vacuum is as inescapable as a black hole. The confession builds trust, yes, but it also reveals a huge character defect; namely, that there isn't any character. If you confess to being a liar, how does that make you honest? The powers that be play this little trick all the time; every "disclosure" is the presentation of an established lie.

In the beginning, there are lies.

Once those lies are let loose, it is impossible to know how much they infect. How far do they reach? How can we say that the fall has affected everything, so much so that the world needed a savior, but the fall has not affected the conditions under which the Bible was written? Of course it has. Creation is fallen. But it's a bit like reading stories about time travel. Cause and effect interweave and blend. It is hard to appreciate that we must discover the fall in a way that is also fallen. Irony is inconceivable. We think that because we are outside the text, we are immune to it. This is not how it works. That text defines, not describes, our world.

This has been well documented over two thousand years. In 312, Constantine converts. While I have enjoyed my life free of persecution, was this really good for the church? Can we really say that Constantine was not influenced by matters of political expediency? Can we really absolve ourselves from all of the abuses that have happened because Christianity was the state religion? The Crusades? The Inquisition? The Holocaust? What about sexual abuse, and the role of religion in racism? As a Christian, I have to ask, would Jesus have wanted any of these institutional sins?

The church has been editing the text from the beginning. At the Council of Nicea in 325, the gospel was canonized and heresies were defined. The books were chosen that went in, and books were chosen that were rejected. But who was right? The year 325 is late to Jesus; those communities were very well established. Were the heretics censored unfairly, or, were they in fact censors themselves? Who was the editor and who was the author? The Gnostics have a very different take on things, a take that is decidedly more dualistic. And they suggest that the creator and creation are evil and that creation is a prison. It might be interesting if that's my thesis, but it's not (although I am strangely captivated by the prison metaphor). My thesis is that there is a painful ambiguity between the tradition and the anti-tradition. Unfortunately, painful ambiguity seems to follow holy mysteries. Would Jesus locate himself in the tradition or the anti-tradition? Is he a critic of the Jewish community, or is he its promised Messiah?

Lies destroy epistemology. Lies destroy how we can know things, and how we can trust. And how we love.

Sometimes people sidestep this by means of dogma. They say "my tradition is pure," and then when that falters they say, "the original intent behind my tradition is pure." Or they say, "I prayed, and because I prayed, I cannot be lied to."

We could just go with the weight and inertia of history. We could say this is how the tradition has carried on for two thousand years, and so it means what they have been saying it meant. That's not sufficient though, if we yoke all Christian spirituality to organized religion, because if we do we have to ask if organized religion has been a system of liberation or a system of control. I realize that my questions and thoughts may create their own binaries, but the discovery of a lie is often the jarring realization that there is more than one interpretation or perspective at work.

Some are scandalized that I am suggesting that there are lies in Scripture. But what do I do when right there at the beginning is tantamount to that disclaimer? The whole book is like the parable of the wheat and tares. A saboteur has snuck in under the cover of darkness, and planted tares in the midst of the harvest. A parable, mind you, that is also Scripture. Again, it would be easy if the whole thing were lies, you could just do the opposite like in the riddle. But what makes it hard is that there is at least as much truth as lies. And we are at a crossroads, like the riddle says. And there couldn't be more riding on this. This is why Joseph Conrad says, "To have his path made clear for him is the aspiration of every human being in our beclouded and tempestuous existence."

8

We have ended the Generation of Polarization—the Score of Schism—running roughly from 9/11 2001 to February of 2020. You could even the score and say September 2021. That was the time between the destruction of the two towers and the pandemic of COVID-19. Cancel culture was born in this time, fraught with all kinds of binary thinking, friending and unfriending, even as it gave a peculiar lip service to nondualism.

Occasionally I will reference things in pop culture, because they are widely accepted markers. I read comic books as a kid, collected them, and was a child of science fiction and fantasy. I would not expect to reference comic books in a project like this, but we have replaced the gods with superheroes for a while now, and there is no point in hiding it.

I really enjoyed the Marvel Comics treatment of exploring 9/11. It was a crossover series called *Civil War*, which explored the American aftermath of 9/11. It was an Orwellian-style exploration, not in the sense of *1984*, but in the sense of *Animal Farm*, where fictional allegory is a useful examination of historical events. Many of these themes were projected onscreen ten years later in a Captain America sequel, and I even published a chapter on that. The chapter was limited in its scope, and I was able to explore this in greater depth in *Christianity and the Art of Wheelchair Maintenance*.

There is a powerful element here that I was not really able to highlight in either treatment. There was promotional art for the comic book series, and the tagline read, "Whose side are you on?" The story really follows Spider-Man. He starts off on Iron Man's side, but finds himself moving over to Captain America's. This gives him the transcendent perspective that is meant for the omniscient reader, and in the movies, this was given to Black Panther.

"Whose side are you on?" It is also a reference to the 1960s cult classic *The Prisoner*. The hero is a spy and he resigns from work only to find himself in the custody of a mysterious captor. Has he been captured by his employer, from whom he quit, or has he been captured by those he has spied upon? He knows too much.

"Whose side are you on?" An answer would be nice, but that would be telling. Every episode opening sequence recreates him demanding to know. He argues against a different voice every time.

That is a good question. It would be nice to tell myself that I am on the side of the Good.

"Whose side are you on?"

We do not know.

But we know we are being lied to.

CHAPTER 3

The Circuit Rider

*I desire to have both heaven and hell ever in my eye,
while I stand on this isthmus of life,
between two boundless oceans.*

JOHN WESLEY

9

By all accounts and by any reckoning I am, first and last, a circuit rider.

What is a circuit rider? I found a hymn written by Methodist preacher Samuel Wakefield in 1854, some sixty years after the death of John Wesley. The hymn is "The Music of His Steps." I wish I had the tune, because without it my brain sets the song to the cadence of "Hickory, dickory, dock." But some of the phrases are so on brand that I think they capture the picture like a country song. There's a reverend with a family and kids, and they loved to hear him come home, "The music of his steps was sought, / His time had come, and he came not . . ." Did you catch that? Dad's not home for dinner. It's a sad song, too, because he never makes it home. This clergyman lives and dies providing ministry to others. Another comes to share, "How died he in a stranger's room, / How strangers laid him in the tomb, / How spake he with his latest breath, / And loved and blessed them all in death."

I remember my own grandmother was sick and recovering, and I was visiting the sick and elderly two states away thinking, "Why am I visiting these sick people, and not my own?" I remember her faith, her smile, her generosity, and her cutting wit. I remember a lot of her phrases and cadences. Her name was Mariah. In contrast, I remember very little of those I visited in my chaplaincy twenty years ago.

When things start to taste bittersweet, you are beginning to understand the circuit rider. At the turn of the century, say between 1850 and 1900, Methodists were very committed to the per capita distribution of their houses of worship. So they would have these itty-bitty communities that could not sustain a pastor. The pastor would be assigned several churches and preach at one in the morning, another in the afternoon, and perhaps another still in the evening. Or the territory would be spread so far that the pastor might show up biweekly or monthly. These pastoral appointments, by the bishop, were known as charges. A three-point charge is a charge with three churches. This is some of the lingo, and it is language that shapes my thinking. American Methodism has a continuum ranging from very high church Anglicanism to the pioneer spirit of the frontier.

By all accounts and any reckoning I am, first and last, a circuit rider. I am a sucker for double *entendre*, which is French for intention. There are reasons for this affinity for puns. But the other sense in which I am a circuit rider is that my wheelchair uses extensive electronics. It's not exactly a "steel horse," but I get where I'm going.

I have all sorts of ambivalences about my wheelchairs. They make my life possible, although life abhors dependency. My own movement is so labored that the liberation afforded by the wheelchair is undeniable (with the annoying exception of the weak battery).

Sometimes I need a new wheelchair. And there are issues with that. First off is that insurance companies won't pay for scooters if you have one already. I would often stash a separate scooter at each point on the charge, because transporting them is difficult. There was a lot of insurance fraud in the 1990s (I still remember the haunting infomercials, "You can get a scooter at no cost to you!"). As a result of which, it became nearly impossible to get a scooter forevermore. The paradox became if you could walk more than ten feet, you couldn't get a scooter. Ten feet? Are you kidding me? Do you realize that the ten-thousand-mile journey starts with the first step?

One of my greatest joys was finding the footprint of Thoreau's cabin. I did this in a scooter. I sat facing Walden Pond, and saw what he saw every morning as he stepped beyond his own threshold. Not the mock-up cabin at the opening to the park, the actual original stones which are pretty much all that are left, and the fireplace. I eventually ran that scooter into the ground, having clean smashed off the front wheel and put it back on only to run it a few years more. That moment was perfect. I understood all the great poets at once—Yeats and the sun-dappled shade, Frost, and Wordsworth's eternal Sylvania. I did not know which was more blue, the water or the sky, and Thoreau proved true again. I was alone, I think as it should be, and I would not have had that moment without the scooter. He left society to live in the woods to learn about life by direct experimentation. He was able to move into his cabin on July 4, Independence Day, and the irony was not lost on him.

I mark the day with fireworks for my kids and remembering him. I have twice made the pilgrimage to Walden and to this soul its waters are more sacred than the Ganges. Tradition prohibits more than one baptism, but if you offered to baptize me in Walden Pond, I just might have to be a heretic.

Of course, he says it best:

> I read in the Gulistan, or Flower Garden, of Sheik Sadi of Shira that "they asked a wise man, saying: Of the many celebrated trees which the Most High God has created lofty and umbrageous, they call none azad, or free, excepting the cypress, which bears no fruit; what mystery is there in this? He replied, Each has its appropriate produce, and appointed season, during the continuance of which it is fresh and blooming, and during their absence dry and withered; to neither of which states is the cypress exposed, being always flourishing; and of this nature are the azads, or religious independents.—Fix not thy heart on that which is transitory; for the Dijlah, or Tigris, will continue to flow through Bagdad after the race of caliphs is extinct: if thy hand has plenty, be liberal as the date tree; but if it affords nothing to give away, be an azad, or free man, like the cypress.

10

My commute is not two way. It never ends. It is, after all, a circuit.

You put in a lot of miles as a circuit rider. The Tao chapter 47 comes to mind here. "Without going outside, you may know the whole world. Without looking through the window, you may see the ways of heaven. The farther you go, the less you know."

The world is only twenty-five thousand miles around, if that. I do that in a year, mostly in Mercer County, tending to my five-point charge. Two acute hospitals, a psychiatric hospital, a hospice, and a nursing home system (that alone had four campuses). On Mondays, I hit the hospital and the church where I meet the students doing nursing home chaplaincy. Tuesday, just the hospital. Wednesday starts with the psychiatric hospital and finishes back over at the main hospital campus. Thursday is just the main campus. Friday is at least half the day on the other side of Trenton. Either Saturday or

Sunday at the psychiatric hospital. Repeat. I'm not listening to Sam Wakefield, but I'd be lying if I said New Jersey's Bon Jovi's "Wanted Dead or Alive" never played on my stereo. Or "Wherever I May Roam." Or "Live This Life." Or "Here I Go Again." This was a routine thing for the Center of Pastoral Care. It was a circuit of vivid beauty and meaning. You would have to be careful avoiding the deer and the jaywalkers both. Seeing pastural lands of New Jersey farms, and the pastoral needs of the soul-sickened suburbs and the dying cities. In this way, I have been around the world more than a dozen times in a Subaru, a Hyundai, and a Dodge Grand Caravan. I am reminded, again, of Shakespeare's King Richard III, "Give me another horse: bind up my wounds!" (Although, in a Mandela effect I remember the quote from Kierkegaard describing Napoleon.)

Chaplaincy has been my window to the world. From inner-city New Jersey hospital rooms I have met someone from every continent. Not just spanning the globe, but spanning the centuries. I have met people touching the last 150 years of history, and possibly the next.

Chaplaincy supervision, that is, running a program of clinical pastoral education, takes this to another degree. As a supervisor, I loved my students. I am forever held to the standards set by Kierkegaard's *Works of Love*. "You shall love your neighbor." That's not just a good idea; that's the Law. So, as a supervisor, I shall love my students. In loving them, I understand them and know them. As I get to know their issues, I get considerable insight into the patients they serve. The students describe their patients' "issues" (a problematic word at best) but these issues are rendered through the "issues" of the students. I would not describe this process as spiritual, although some may, and what emerges is a kind of trigonometry between the chaplain and patient. Through this trigonometry, I find myself in the dialectical position to love chaplain and patient more. To know them more.

"Without going outside, you may know the whole world."

11

My space is the space between.

I am ordained clergy. I was commissioned as a deacon in the United Methodist Church in 2003. John Wesley himself had a wandering soul and he ventured into controversial spaces like the scandal of outdoor preaching. He famously said, "The world is my parish." That sounds like a chaplain to me. This was under the 1996 *Book of Discipline*. At the time, the denomination was trying to do something especially creative with the diaconate, by instituting an order of "permanent deacon" because most Christian groups use the order of deacon as a transitional phase to the full priesthood. But what if someone became a deacon, and stayed that way?

The deacon was ordained to word and service. The elder was ordained to word, service, order, and sacrament. I understood this to be a focused specialization. Deacons have since whined and complained, and now they're ordained to four things too. But the idea was they needed the extra bandwidth to span their position. They had one foot solidly in the church and one foot in the world. It was a bridge ordination. And it was an ordination ideal for the structure of chaplaincy.

The irony is that deacons are not supposed to itinerate. Which means they are not moved at the direction of the bishop. Deacons find their employment independently, and then they are appointed. Elders itinerate, and go wherever the bishop sends them. In the last fifty years this has relaxed considerably because of the reality of families and two-income families and things like that. But the elder vow is to go where the bishop sends you. The itinerate ministry fits in with the concept of the circuit rider. Somehow, even as a deacon I find myself itinerant still.

My entire chaplaincy is marked by these two worlds. As a seminarian in my first year I was a full-time student in the academy and a part-time chaplain at a nursing home. In my second year, I was split between a homeless shelter and hospital. In my third year, the VA and the academy. Up in Philadelphia, my residency involved a split between psychiatric and acute hospital care. And then, when I started chaplaincy in Trenton, I was split between two campuses across town. This was all before the Center for Pastoral Care, which became its own five-point charge.

My space is the space between.

CHAPTER 4

The Margins

I have no doubt that some of you who read this book
are unable to pay for all the dinners which you have actually eaten,
or for the coats and shoes which are fast wearing or are already worn out,
and have come to this page to spend borrowed or stolen time,
robbing your creditors of an hour.
It is very evident what mean and sneaking lives many of you live,
for my sight has been whetted by experience;
always on the limits,
trying to get into business and trying to get out of debt,
a very ancient slough, called by the Latins *aes alienum*,
another's brass, for some of their coins were made of brass;
still living, and dying, and buried by this other's brass;
always promising to pay, promising to pay, tomorrow,
and dying today, insolvent . . .

THOREAU, EMPHASIS MINE

12

One of my favorite depictions of John Wesley is on horseback. Horses are in themselves beautiful animals that have much to teach, and I have spent some time with riding programs for the disabled. But my connection is something else. I like the depiction on horseback because Wesley is reading a Bible. All of this is antiquated. Horses are antiquated (although they are the first self-driving car). Books and literacy are antiquated (although this image is the prototype of texting while driving). Maybe even the Bible is antiquated (not because I don't love it, but because I do). But the image is iconic enough that any Methodist would recognize it, and when you are going from point "A" to point "B" you can do something else. Maybe stronger still when you are going from point "A" to point "B" you must do something else. Maybe when you are going from point "A" to point "B" a space will emerge, and into that space something must materialize. You can daydream, you can stare at the back end of the horse in front of you, or you can leverage the margin.

My heart becomes strangely warmed at the thought of Wesley's sermon on "Redeeming the Time," which itself is a beautiful phrase hoping too that even time may be redeemed.

13

Thoreau brings in a monetized sense of the margin, and those limits are very much a part of this conversation. All limits constrain and intersect into even more constrained sectors. Bonhoeffer famously said as a seminary student that he didn't want to be rich, he just didn't want to have to worry about paying for lunch for fear of running out of money. He "didn't want to have to count." The irony that the young man did not see that the old man surely did is that it is only the rich who get to have lunch and not worry about where it's coming from. Everyone else has to count. This, too, is the myth of better and worse. Surely someone is comfortably in the middle; that is, more comfortable than me, but not the evil rich. I don't have to be at the top, goes the faux-negotiation, but I don't want to be at the bottom. Middle managers are not comfortable; all you have to do is talk to one and you discover that. The fantasy is that you could have this infinitely wide and infinitely comfortable middle class. No pyramid is built like that, and such is utterly impossible. More on that later.

A few words on what is the margin, and what the margin is not. I am prone to polyvalent words, but it is prudent to provide a partial unpacking.

We might think of margins or limits as bad. This is not right. A bad thing happened between the 1.44 MB floppy and the CD-ROM (which held 700 MB). Coding got really sloppy when programs no longer had to fit on a disk. It had been tight and elegant, but quickly became bloated and unstable. A complete lost cause when patches were available for download.

A margin can be that which is benefit, such as a profit margin. The business was successful because the margins were good.

A margin can be that which is negligible, such as a marginal loss. He made a marginal impact.

One of my most beloved senses of the word are the margins of a page. There is the place on the page where you are supposed to write, and places where you are not—for various reasons. On school paper, the lines are actually printed.

The academy has taught me that being "marginalized" makes me a victim. If my perspective has been relegated to the margins, then I don't have power or voice. Like a peculiar and ironic taxidermist, the academy has sought to collect and mount marginalized groups for preservation. The newest group is "disability." It is important to note that "disability" did not exist in academic print a hundred years ago, although one could find the religious category of "suffering." In that category, I am in the majority and soon you will join me if not already. Perhaps, here, it may help to reach out to bell hooks: "Understanding marginality as position and place of resistance is crucial for oppressed, exploited, colonized people. If we only view the margin as sign marking the despair, a deep nihilism penetrates in a destructive way the very ground of our being." And what if the greatest colonist of all has been Plato's academy?

Life has taught me that there is great power in the margins. The margins are Briar Rabbit's briar patch—that place no one wants to go, but a place where I enjoy great freedom. Do you know the story? Briar Rabbit is about to be lynched or killed, and he begs his stupid captors to not throw him into the briar patch, which they do because they desire cruelty above all else. But Briar Rabbit is perfectly at home in the patch, that's his namesake after all, and he escapes easily.

It is an interesting detour for a moment, to think about Briar Rabbit and Disney's *Song of the South* through which Briar Rabbit was immortalized before being canceled. The author of Briar Rabbit was born in 1844, twenty years before the Civil War. He was White, yes, but sought to give voice to a marginalized folklore. A full hundred years later, in 1944, the movie was made, itself twenty years before the civil rights movement. The film intentionally depicts real or imagined progressive values of Whites aspiring to be less racist. I should also underscore that every studio makes movies to be successful—that is, to make money. And it did. Today, the studio attempts to leverage its branding by standing against its earlier work. Taken just a little further, you could easily say the studio hopes to assert more dominance in the marketplace of ideas (through which additional successful movies might be made), by standing against its former project—something undeniably progressively liberating. The facts are the facts; the story has not changed. Briar Rabbit still has a Black accent, and will continue to do so—until the remake. But the business end of the weapon has changed. The tip of the spear is now the handle. This is how the battle is waged. It is a battle in time, through time, and about time. Deliverance is changed into oppression and back again. Somehow, light is changed into shadow. It is quaint to think that this is random. "The times are changing. Culture is evolving." As if the one had nothing to do with the other. Yes, stories do randomly fall in and out of fashion. It is also supremely naïve to dismiss the inversion and perversion of hero into demon when we are so obviously and utterly polarized in our thinking.

You can see these things from the margin.

14

Among many things, a disability is a huge waste of time. Do not be disabled when you are in a hurry. The disability interacts with the marginal life in a particularly complicated way. I can cut corners to save time. I can walk less to use the wheelchair more, which is faster, but doing so diminishes my exercise and health. The moral of this delightful story is that I have to run through my day both as quickly and as strenuously all the time and if I fail to do either I have to pay the difference. I have to do as many difficult things as I can in a way as difficult as possible, all the time, every day. And time is a factor. It is the impossible, as impossibly as possible. This is worse than the zero-sum game, where all of the shortcuts perfectly cancel my health. It's like having a really huge number, like 31 trillion, 31,000,000,000,000, and multiplying that by zero.

Still, the urge to cut corners is irresistible. It was at the beginning of this part of my ministry that I began to shave my head. Shaving my head was easier than washing and combing my hair, and I could do this at traffic lights, and if I couldn't and had to skip a day of shaving no one complained. It is a peculiar asceticism. It is as if my birthday suit has been replaced by a hair shirt. If there is something that I can do in a way that is faster and/or doesn't hurt, somewhere along the line I will pay for it, and pay dearly. I have to do things as uncomfortably as possible, because if I don't there will be more pain later and lost ability.

The combined toll on my time (between the margins and the disability itself) is enormous. You won't make it. My wheelchair and rider has been left behind on more than one platform. The conductor can't even see me.

We all feel the slow crunch of wasted time; I'm not unique in that. I've no sole right to the claim of frustration. We have all spent hours of life, so numerous as to make the slow creep on eternity, on hold waiting for some specialist to answer what is a very simple but specific question. We have all felt the collective inefficiency of the digital age become asymptotically evil and the only description is bondage. We are all doing time, from one insurance claim (insurance that I pay for) to the next.

But in such an absurd world, with disability, somehow, everything is harder. Everything takes longer. Dressing, undressing, eating, showering, anything, typing.

When I'm in a new environment, I have to block out the space, as if I were a competitive dancer who trained on one stage, but must perform on another of differing dimensions. "Let's see, grab there, step there, turn there."

Think of all the times you do two things at once. Now think about doing that with one hand. The world of multitasking becomes an agonizing series.

When your wheelchair is left on the platform along with that which sits in it, you have a lot of time to think about things.

15

The wardens and the guards with their towers and their yards do not like what happens in the margin. Floodlight may break the night, spotlight might burn with spite, but the margin may they never take. The margin is my own, this old dog his bone, and in it, I but my God am alone. At last free, first I see that which is mine is me. Moon may shine; my soul is mine, meant for Thine, in the margin be. The wardens and the guards with their towers and their yards do not like what happens in the margin.

I'm not kidding when I say the wardens and the guards do not like what happens in the margin. They hate it, because the margin is the space no one can touch. They find it with fury and outrage, and this will often spill into violence and a thirst for cruelty. "How dare you?!" Livid. That's when they really want to hurt you and make sure you got the message. Livid because in the margin I am free, livid because deep within in their margin they know they are not. This thing that is my key is their lock. "How dare you have that? How dare you have any joy?! How dare you, of all people, try to oppose me? Believe me when I tell you: I will hit you so hard your grandchildren will feel it."

Perhaps. I have been hit before. I can be hurt.

Philosopher and psychoanalyst Victor Frankl wrote *Man's Search for Meaning* in the camps, literally in the margins—scraps of paper even. But the power of a book is not on the pages. The power is in the soul of the author, and in the hearts of his readers however few they be. It is a quantum power, shaping probability fields of what can happen. It is a spiritual power, generating hope and movement. We remember Victor Frankl. Not one guard has a name.

Tragically, the thing happened exactly as he feared. The book was found by the Nazis. He was punished. Of course, it was destroyed. Of course, he wrote it again, and published it to the world.

This document very much exists as a marginal exercise. It is my rock hammer and I Dufresne. I chip away every chance I get, with the one hand that works. I do not know if I will finish, or if it will finish me. I do not know if anyone will ever read this. This is my note stuffed into the wall. This is my inch by inch. I did a short project on *V for Vendetta*, too—a great prison movie.

Nobody has asked me to write this. I know this is not so different from any book. But there is no room in my life for any of this, and as I write these words about margins that irony is not lost on me. I hope there is a you that smiles here, too. You understand that I did this for me. But I hope you share this. This is my message in the bottle. And thank you.

The wardens and the guards with their towers and their yards do not like what happens in the margin. Floodlight may break the night, spotlight might burn with spite, but the margin may they never take. The margin is my own, this old dog his bone, and in it, I but my God am alone. At last free, first I see that which is mine is me. Moon may shine; my soul is mine, meant for Thine, in the margin be. The wardens and the guards with their towers and their yards do not like what happens in the margin.

16

I was pulled over on the road from Pennington to Hopewell. As if it were biblical, that is the name of the road. This is not uncommon. You get pulled for lots of things in Hopewell. When I would drive the babies to sleep in the middle of the night when they were weaning I would get pulled over just for being out late. Then, the question is can the officer turn off the lights before the baby wakes. The question is, is the officer ready to deal with a crying baby.

This was different. "Do you know why I pulled you over?"

This is always a trick question for me. I was so tied up with my ministry circuit that it was impossible to keep everything current. There are headlights, tail lights, broken mirrors, inspection stickers. So you don't want to offer too much. And, this circuit rider is not slow.

"Um, no. I'm sorry, officer, what's the problem?"

"You were over the white line."

"The *white* line? I'm worried about the *yellow* line." That part of the shoulder on that stretch is well faded and worn. It's practically a supplemental lane. The worst thing over there is broken asphalt and road debris. If you hit something there it's just another bad day. It's the yellow line that gets you killed.

I have made a marginal life over the white line, living the dialectic between death and a bad day. I think about the white line. A lot. I walk the line. My thoughts turn to the *barzakh*, an Islamic isthmus between heaven and hell. My thoughts turn to the *bardo*, a Buddhist concept between death and rebirth. *Barzakh* and *bardo* blessed be.

I got the citation. Also a bad day.

CHAPTER 5

The Exodus

> And it came to pass in process of time,
> that the king of Egypt died:
> and the children of Israel sighed by reason of the bondage,
> and they cried,
> and their cry came up unto God by reason of the bondage.
> And God heard their groaning,
> and God remembered his covenant
> with Abraham, with Isaac, and with Jacob.
> And God looked upon the children of Israel,
> and God had respect unto them.
>
> THE BOOK OF EXODUS

17

Imagine a prison. Now imagine that prison on an island, surrounded by shark-infested waters. I love prison movies like *The Shawshank Redemption* and I would count *The Truman Show* in this number. The scenario I'm describing ought to remind you of *Escape from Alcatraz* if you've seen it.

The problem is twofold. The problem is that you are a prisoner, yes, but also that there is nowhere to go. It's doubly difficult. Perhaps you could overthrow the guards (but they have all the guns and power), or perhaps you could simply escape (but you have no boat and nowhere to go). Either one of these are valid solutions, and either one of these conditions (captivity or isolation) is enough to keep you prisoner.

This is a great scenario. A scenario like this can teach you many things about the human condition, about what it means to be alive, and what it means to be free. I would pay good money to see a thoughtful treatment of this story.

In many ways this is the scenario we find in the Bible. That is, what I've been describing to you is the story of Exodus. The Hebrews are a thoroughly conquered people, in bondage to the Egyptians. The Egyptians hold a lot of power here and may be the global superpower depending on what era of Mesopotamia we are considering.

Moreover, there's nowhere to go. When you are surrounded by an impossible desert, you can't just flee your captors.

But one more thing . . . this is where Steve Jobs comes in.

18

Before I get into Steve Jobs, I want to celebrate just how archetypical and prototypical the exodus is. It is everything—but typical. It is the type of all types.

The call and response of Moses will shape how we think about the spiritual life altogether. We call it the "walk with God." Because Genesis will talk about how Enoch and Noah walked with God, but we get that idiom from Moses. It is this great sojourn into the desert, by foot, that becomes the very metaphor for the spiritual life. This is huge. The Hebrew word for this is *Halacha*, which means walk and is used unsurprisingly to refer to the Law of Moses. The language here has some pliability. Moses "walks" through the desert, and this sojourn becomes the "walk with God."

There is something about the asceticism of the desert. In the desert water finds sacred meaning far beyond the water of the Nile. In the desert we see the Red Sea divided like the wet from dry in creation itself, or water being cleft from the rock and the staff of Moses. Because the desert is a lonely place, but so lonely that it will be burned into the tradition as the place where Jesus will go for self-care.

For a moment I think about the beauty of the Lord's Prayer. This is probably Jesus at his most pedagogical. His disciples have asked him how should we pray? And he says give us this day our daily bread. "Give us this day our daily bread." This is not some pragmatic advice or token acknowledgment of material need. This is an unfootnoted reference to the exodus itself, the great journey from Egypt and the manna from heaven that made it possible.

There is much to be said about the exodus.

Steve Jobs said, "You're born alone, and you die alone." Moses thinks like an abandoned person. He is the Steve Jobs of his day. Steve Jobs said, "You are born alone, and you die alone." I really liked that statement when I first heard it. I'll go a little further and add that my wife was horrified by the statement. Orson Welles said something even darker, which is, "You are born alone, you live alone, and you die alone," which touches on the problem of being and existence. So it seems that Steve gave Orson a good old Apple upgrade and streamlined it to birth and death. The sentence is, of course, both true and false. It is impossible for anyone to be born alone, flat out. But at the same time, it is equally impossible that anyone else could ever get between us and these intense experiential parentheses of life; that is, no one except God.

I invoke Steve Jobs of Apple Computer because he's our present-day example of out-of-the-box thinking. It's unimaginable. Jobs was renowned for creating a personal "reality-distortion field" where he would continually exhort his creative team to create the impossible. It had never been done before and there was no way to do it. To paraphrase Joseph Campbell: How do you know it's your path? Because it's under your feet. It was awesome and fearsome, and they had a lot of things to say about Jobs as a person that weren't very flattering.

But let it be said that Moses was able to think like Steve Jobs. He is able to envision new possibilities that no one else seriously wants to consider. Yes, you can leave Egypt. You really can. We look at the narrative and we see things the way we like to look. We come up with phrases like a foot in two worlds, and we don't see the deeper experience. We are like children who easily become jealous, and when our friend tells us about the reality of family divorce, all we can think to ourselves is it must be nice to have two Christmases.

What we are overlooking and ignoring is what it really means to have a foot in two worlds. It doesn't mean you have two houses. It means you are homeless. Or, perhaps more broadly, that you are "home free," or more broadly even still, that the whole world is your home and that you are always home. Or maybe even that the "whole world is your parish." But this is getting ahead of things.

These themes have always powerfully attracted me to the Scriptures of Moses. There are little points of connection to the story, a speech impediment and difficulty in public speaking. I can identify with that. But more substantially, there is the connection of two worlds and the in-between space. Tradition holds that Moses was Hebrew and his mother placed him in the Nile River. There he was found by the daughter of Pharaoh in the house of Pharaoh, and there you have it: two worlds.

Before you think I'm making too much of it, let it be said that most scholars and interpreters have made too little. Because a couple of lines later, Moses actually goes out and kills an Egyptian—ostensibly for mistreating other Hebrews. This bicultural experience weighed heavily on Moses, throughout his adolescence, and eventually brought him to a place where he could become capable of murder. This murderous act propels Moses to go and hide, and leave everything he has known, and he goes and starts a new life, and becomes a father, and sees that another way is possible.

Through the story of Moses we see a man who is called by God. This calling of God, although placed near the beginning of Scripture, is not the only call story. There are many. God calls out to Adam and Eve, out to Abraham, Noah, even Cain. It is repeated in Scripture, this call and response pattern between God and those chosen. But there is something that manifests in the Moses story that becomes illustrative of a theme and tendency. God calls, and Moses responds, "Here I am, Lord." You could even say that his "dominant response" is "Here I am, Lord." And the conversation unfolds and the dialogue continues, the divine back and forth of it all. And very quickly Moses will ask the divine existential questions. "Who am I?" and "Who are You?" Or, at least, "Who shall I say who sent me?" and God will answer, rest assured, "I AM."

Do you see it? The progression of the dialogue mirrors the progression of the journey.

What happens next in this string and stream of back and forth is nothing less than the archetype of epic. It is a series of events that it is so definitive for these people of Abraham (who had his own call and dominant response with God) that the Moses epic will weave itself into the fabric of the Ten Commandments. In fact, they will begin with the instruction to remember that the entire religious tradition and law was born out of a call and response, and a journey truly of epic proportion. It goes "Remember that I the Lord your God who brought you out of Egypt . . ." And it goes on from there into Law. And for a moment we pause and recognize that even though today we want to argue Law and ask if it includes these people, or those people, we forget that it begins with the divine instruction to remember that all of this begins with a calling. And a response, and a journey.

Note well, it is not only the archetype of the epic; it is also the archetype of the "Holy Dialogue."

Moses answers the call, and Moses does the unthinkable, and leads everyone, even the women and children, into the desert. And we try to simplify things, and upgrade everything, and skip to the end although doing so is profoundly stupid because in God there is no end. And we are quick to label this as the story of how Moses gets to the promised land. Except that in many ways, that's not what the story is. Because, really, Moses never gets to the promised land, only to see it. And when I was a child I thought this was so unfair, and such a "close but no cigar" and only at middle age did I understand that Moses has been given much better. Moses has seen the glory of God, proven time and again, and what greater blessing could there be?

It is there in the desert that we begin to see how this all works. It is there where we begin to see what the ministry of Moses is all about. I like to see him as the prototype of the first chaplain, and we see that his work is not so much transportation as it is transformation. It is there in the desert that we understand what it takes to transform a people, and that true deliverance can never happen without true transformation. Chaplaincy retains this peripatetic mission: we walk with the patients through their suffering. And in circumambulating the sacred like a holy labyrinth, that walk also becomes our walk with God.

CHAPTER 6

The Traveler's Cloak

> My clothing is a Scythian cloak,
> my shoes are the hard soles of my feet,
> my bed is the earth,
> my food is only seasoned by hunger—
> and I eat nothing but milk and cheese and meat.
> Come and visit me, and you will find me at peace.
> You want to give me something.
> But give it to your fellow-citizens instead,
> or let the immortal gods have it.
>
> ANACHARSIS

19

What you may not know is that every chaplain has a traveler's cloak.

Anacharsis may be the first to embody exactly the ruggedness here. It seems like he was from New Jersey. There is something crass here. But when the passerby says "up yours," you can sense it's still affectionate. In New York, the inference is "up yours (and die)." My friend from Long Island helped me parse that out.

It is hard for me to convey how important Anacharsis was. Today, he is swallowed by time, all but erased completely. In his time, he was considered one of the Seven Sages of Greece and this is huge. He wasn't even Greek. He was Scythian. Think Iran and Persia. Another thing is that all Seven Sages lived in the 600s (BC) and so their ideas created the conceptual fabric for the 500s, which is a very important time, what Karl Jaspers calls the Axial Age when the modern religions were born and the biblical prophets lived. It's the Axial Age that will germinate the genius of Socrates.

Across my studies, Anacharsis is the first in the history of philosophy to document the traveler's cloak, especially this kind of Platonic traveler's cloak that may not be a literal cloak at all. Anacharsis is adorned in an attitude.

In my own silly story, I was not introduced to the traveler's cloak by Anacharsis who lived 2,600 years ago. I first heard of the cloak in *Kung Fu*, the 1970s television series with David Carradine. I'm not going to lie, I love that series. The cloak comes up in an episode called "The Soul is the Warrior." One of the masters invites our hero to take "the traveler's cloak that shelters and protects."

The series premiered a few months after I was born. It is the perfect chaplain epic. By genre, it's a Western. It's a very popular example of the "walk-the-earth" trope. Indeed, this is even named by Quentin Tarantino (who also loved David Carradine) in his *Pulp Fiction* and the show is mentioned in one of Samuel L. Jackson's soliloquies. The trope is a staple of the "hero's journey." We see three years of the story proper, three years of childhood flashbacks, and three years of adolescence. It's an epic. This was very popular in the 1960s with *Route 66* and *The Fugitive*. We see it again in the 1970s in shows like *Kung Fu* and *The Incredible Hulk*. In the 1980s, it was *Knight Rider* (a young loner on a crusade to champion the cause of the innocent, the helpless, the powerless in a world of criminals who operate "above the law"). The hero has a quest, and a problem, and chooses to serve those around him. To be their champion. This was how my imagination was formed.

Unlike *The Incredible Hulk*, the hero has no power. He only has his spirituality. He is a Buddhist/Taoist monk. He says he's Buddhist but only Taoist texts are quoted across the series. In *The Fugitive*, the hero is innocent and must run from episode to episode to prove his innocence. In *Kung Fu*, the monk enters the story as guilty. He really has killed a man. And for the entire series, he will atone for his sin. His name is Kaine. Yeah. Like the biblical Cain. At full circle, he says, "I follow the Tao. No one can say to what solitude that might lead. My journey is endless until it comes full circle at my death."

Kafka has a beautiful parable about this. A noble hears a trumpet in the distance. His squire does not. The noble hears a calling, and immediately takes his horse on a journey. He takes no provisions, because it will be impossible to carry everything he'll need. His destination? "Away-from-here." I share this parable with every class of chaplains.

What Kafka's getting at is the subtle distinction between those who are on the journey, and those who are not. Thoreau begins his *magnum opus* with a fetching turn of phrase. He describes "the sojourner in civilized life." People thought he was strange because he was a sojourner to the woods, but there is something so much more honest about life there that his sense of space was inverted and he was a sojourner in civilized life. That was my experience of Las Vegas at a chaplaincy convention in 2013. The beauty of the desert enwreathed the city like an inverted oasis, itself a shabby place of thirst, burn, and hunger.

I have become something of a hermit. I did not plan on becoming a hermit. Maybe we could say a hermit in a civilized life. Thoreau's sojourner is not at home where he goes; thus the sojourn.

How is it that you are not at home with everyone else? You are a person on a planet of people, how can this be?

There are many reasons in my life how this came to be, and I will share as many as I can. But the important thing is that when I picked up the traveler's cloak, I stopped *trying* to be at home with everyone else.

I use the word *hermit* to denote the assumed loneliness. It is not lonely. But it is different. Most people are terrified by different. My thoughts jump back to the existentialist Victor Frankl, who says, "To exist is to be different." To be the one that is different must be lonely, they think.

How is it different? I talk with people I don't know for a living. I once met the absurdist Steven Wright, who said, "I like to reminisce with people I don't know"—and I actually do. But at the Girl Scout event where the moms are gathered, I have nothing to say. It's like I can't talk if there's not a dead body in the room. It's not that I don't have thoughts, or that I'm unwilling to share my inner experiences, or even that I don't enjoy the inner experiences of others. It's that I can't do the small talk. I don't go anywhere where you are not allowed to talk politics or religion, because those are the only things I talk about. The problem may well be that I very much do enjoy sharing the inner experience of others, and it is precisely the point of small talk to negate this possibility. In fact, much of basic training is teaching chaplains to not try to bond by socializing and chitchat.

Why is my talking different? Well, lots of reasons. I'm sure the amount of time I'm thinking about either death or God has something to do with it. It's hard not to be flippant about it. Because the torque of it all is not that it's special, and certainly not that I'm so important on my special task thinking about special things. It's that it's exquisitely ordinary. We are all surrounded by death and God all the time. You watch a lot of people die, for sure. You see a lot of change that is both in an instant and a process. I once explained to a friend, "It's like being a priest of unanswered prayers." The reader should know: we don't talk any more.

It is essential that the traveler's cloak be simple. It can't be ornate or any kind of finery. I like Thoreau's gloss of Plato on Socrates, "It is desirable that a man be clad so simply that he can lay his hands on himself in the dark, and that he live in all respects so compactly and preparedly that, if an enemy take the town, he can, like the old philosopher, walk out the gate empty-handed without anxiety."

Scripture captures this. Jesus is sending out the disciples and it says in Mark 6, "And he commanded them that they should take nothing for their journey, save a staff only; no scrip, no bread, no money in their purse: But be shod with sandals; and not put on two coats." The RSV says "tunics" for "coats." Sometimes I refer to this verse as the "anti-two tunic clause."

It could just as well say cloaks. Jesus is not saying that the gospel is to become a mendicant. Rather, if you are going to take up this journey, you absolutely must discover and access resources much greater than yourself, far more than you can carry. Quite simply, you are going to have to learn how to trust.

The traveler's cloak is important. One traveler's cloak is essential. Two is what the Tao calls "extra food and unnecessary luggage. They do not bring happiness."

20

I did my chaplaincy training through the Association of Clinical Pastoral Education. But I began my ministry in chaplaincy supervision through the College of Pastoral Supervision and Psychotherapy. I traveled the crooked line, and I'll try to straighten that out before I finish. But I have been a most circuitous circuit rider.

The CPSP has this covenantal value of "traveling light." It's a mission statement about prioritizing people over principles and purpose over bureaucracy. I'll confess, this can be very, very attractive. By now, you know my penchant for wordplay. I hear the meaning differently each time. Today, I hear that as traversing across or along beams of light. But this is not my normative connotation. I often think about the gravelly tones of Leonard Cohen, who has a song by the same name. Cohen the poet priest sings descriptively of younger and wilder days. In this tune, he makes it clear that his mind is set on leaving and leaving the table. Where is he going? "Away-from-here," although in this bard's parlance that might be better named "back-to-You." Indeed, one may well have to travel light for a grand destiny like that.

21

What is the good of a traveler's cloak?

The cloak allows you to love, and to say goodbye. Forever.

The cloak allows you to give, and you have more than before.

The cloak allows you to respect suffering, and even more to respect the sufferer. Without pity.

To know and to not know.

To speak the unspeakable and to hear the ineffable.

It gives you access to hidden places.

To be awkward and not care what others think.

To not take things that do not belong to you. And certainly to not take them home.

To be cold. To be hungry. To be tired. To be frustrated. Most people call this patience.

To truly serve without any regard for appreciation or advantage.

To feel everything. Even fear.

To love without attachment and with unbridled, passionate compassion.

To be without anxiety.

To pray.

22

What do I mean when I say every chaplain has a traveler's cloak?

No, they don't hand them out. Maybe they should, but invariably someone would misplace it. The current system of distribution is much better.

Most people think that "chaplain" is related to "chapel." It's not. Distant cousin at best.

The word "chaplain" comes from the Latin *capella*. As in, "cape." It's even more apparent in the Spanish, *Capellan*. Legend has it that Martin of Tours needed to cleft his cloak in twain. He was a soldier before a bishop, and with a sword stroke he shared his cloak with a beggar in snow. On the road—where chaplains belong. The word chapel was later applied to the structure where Martin's cloak was kept as a relic. On an interesting note, Matthew and Mark have versions of the "anti-two tunic clause." In Luke, it says if you have two, give the second to one who needs it. Martin seems to do one better, almost creating it *ex nihilo*.

We are named for the traveler's cloak. You reference it every time you say my name.

CHAPTER 7

The Adoption

Here among the graves in the twilight
I see one thing only, but I see that thing clear.
I see the long wall of a rampart sombre with sunset,
a dusty road at its base.
On the tower of the rampart stand the glorious high gods,
Death and the rest, insolent and watching.
Below on the road stream the tribes of men,
tired, bent, hurt, and stumbling,
and each man alone.
As one comes beneath the tower,
the High God descends and faces the wayfarer.
He speaks three slow words: "Who are you?"
The pilgrim I know should be able to straighten his shoulders,
to stand his tallest, and to answer defiantly,
"I am your son."

WILLIAM ALEXANDER PERCY

23

So, another thing that I share in common with Moses, aside from being in two worlds, and aside from a speech impediment, is that I am adopted. This is also something I share with Steve Jobs. It was in an article on his adoption where I found the quote about being born alone.

This has also been a fact of my entire life; that is, it is something you live with. I was born in 1972, and then the conventional wisdom was to not tell children that they were adopted. I think that this is a dimension of our culture's delusional fantasy that the story you choose for yourself is the only thing that matters. For myself, I began to understand this, my adoption, when I was eight. Maybe nine. Right around *The Empire Strikes Back*. Just like Luke Skywalker.

I thought I knew what it meant, all throughout my life. I thought I understood the fullness of its meaning, even though the meaning continued to grow and swell beyond all expectation. It is hard to describe what it means. The preadolescent discovery of adoption is difficult. We've all had the experiences of being lied to and that never feels good. But the adoptee also bears the fate of having been completely wrong about the most basic facts of life, such as mother and father and sister, and where one comes from. The error is profoundly confusing and shocking. You discover that the nightmare of a child is actually true.

There are also many imagined interpretations and questions that the adoptee will have to hold. Why was I rejected? Why was I abandoned? What does it mean to be utterly and profoundly estranged? What was wrong with me? Why am I disposable? Was I stolen? Are there people looking for me? Does someone out there love me? Does anyone love me? Who am I? Where do I come from?

Adoption is many things. For one woman adoption is the determined resolve that "I will not let that social worker take my baby," even as she will come back to the hospital the very next day in order to sign the papers. For another woman, adoption is the letter to the social worker that God "needs me to take care of this baby," and only when she discovers that he is special needs.

24

Honestly, it wasn't until my recent ministry at the psychiatric hospital where I really appreciated the vastness of meaning around adoption. My favorite unit is the Adult Psychiatric & Addiction Unit, or APA, or Dual Diagnosis Unit. These patients very much live in the same worlds as you and I, but their lives are broken open so far that the whole world can see. They live in complexity, with multiple problems that are all in conflict with each other. They have so many problems that even their problems have problems.

But I was shocked when I learned how many of these patients were adopted or had some kind of foster parent. And they reported a vivid and visceral experience of alienation so intense that I recognized it both in horror and comfort. They reported an experience of feeling extremely different from everyone else. Some described a bodily felt hole. Others described rejection, alienation. And, after living a lifetime with these powerful and powerfully sad feelings, they came to believe the meaning of these feelings was that they were bad and beyond hope.

You may have noticed that I said that I recognized it in horror and comfort. The comfort was a strange one, because I never knew—never, despite my ministry and my training—that other people actually felt this way. I too have lived with this sense of being extremely different from everyone else, but I thought I knew what it meant. And I was shocked as I took it all in.

I'll need to explain it by analogy. As it turns out, psychosis is more pervasive among people who are deaf than those who are blind. This surprises many of us who are gifted with both senses because we imagine it easier to live deaf than blind, because we are so dependent on what we think we see. But developmentally, it turns out that blindness is easier to grow up with than deafness. The proposed explanation for this is that blind people have a context for things, a soundtrack if you will, to their very lives. They hear people approach and walk away. For the deaf, they turn around and people appear and disappear. They live without the fabric of context.

And today, I think my disability saved me, saved me from the same fate of problematic adoption and abandonment that so many people on the APA unit have. I grew up and I felt completely different from the whole world, living in two worlds, and homeless like Ishmael. And I thought that the reason for that feeling was embedded in my body. Not only did I feel different, but I looked different. And not only could I see it, but so could everybody else. I had a context, like the blind man, for why I felt this way, and I think this allowed me to develop a self esteem because I could associate all these negative feelings with my disability, and then imagine myself apart from my disability and imagine myself more than my disability.

But that's just me. I'm not qualified to define disability or adoption for anyone else. I only want to share with you the way that the meaning of my life has slowly unfolded before me, and continues to do so, and will continue into my future. For most of my life, I could only understand myself in the terms that I was given, and even as we were all forced into the language of political correctness, I could only see my disability as a physical challenge to be overcome, and never possibly receive it as a saving grace.

The very facts and accidents in the stories of our lives are inherently meaningful, especially the accidents that are ugly and those that we are quick to overlook, or those that we think we understand. I believe that the fact that Moses lived in two worlds was an essential accident, upon which the rest of the narrative is based and predicated. It is that core experience of abandonment that gives him a murderous passion for social justice, and it is the same experience that gives him the ability to think new thoughts, and to go into the wilderness that no one else would choose, to allow himself to hear the voice and calling of God.

His core experience, especially of being of two worlds, is one that will profoundly shape his thinking. It will mark him. Body, mind, and spirit. And this experience is so profound, so formative on his future life, these seemingly meaningless details are cut forever into Scripture. This is important because we want to forget how the details of a story can shape you. We have ideas about adoption and politics about adoption, even theology about adoption, and we want to believe that the only story that matters for us is the one we make up. But that's not how it works. That's not how meaning works, and that's not how life works.

This requires a little explaining to the uninitiated. The uninformed perspective is inclined to confuse reciprocal needs versus complementary needs. In some kind of Woody Allen equivocation, you can shrug your shoulders and say, "Needs are needs." But they are not. Needs have meaning and you don't get to ignore meaning just because it is ugly or messes up the story you want to tell. A baby needs care; adoptive parents need a baby. That's a complementary need. But we ignore the reality of the mother-baby bond. That's a reciprocal need because both parties say, "I need you." Is that true? Ask any mother. Does it matter if we forcibly transpose the complementary need over the reciprocal one? Well, we can, and we certainly like to. But reality is pernicious. The adoptive couple has a fertility problem; the baby severed from mother (and father); the mother bereft. Generally speaking, all three of the stories won't tolerate each other. Someone is going to get their story denied and possibly all three will. What does it mean? It very well could mean that this baby who has come to believe that he is abandoned is unable to ever really satisfy the unconscious longing of the couple's fertility issues. That's a bad mix.

Of course the meaning is not locked into one of three perspectives, like the play *Rashaman*. Meaning abounds. Yes, there is the meaning that is found, the meaning that is forced, and the meaning that is chosen. But there is also the hand of God—which always seems to contain a wild card. With the adoption of Moses, mother and baby are reunited. The adoptive Egyptian mother needs a wet nurse. And in my own life, I was incredibly blessed in my adoption. My mother and father both unknowingly took on and loved and supported a special needs child with a disability that is likely a birth trauma. That disability was unknown to them. When discovered, they saw purpose. "Maybe this child needs me." Which, I did.

25

Early on, I fell in love with epigrams in front of chapters. Sentences derive meaning from the dialectical relations and positions and forms of their words. You could even say the same about words and letters. Paragraphs are literally literary pictures—graphs—that are arranged and positioned to build ideas. Ideas can then be juxtaposed to their chapter titles, and these can then be set into contrast against their epigram. I do creative nonfiction which is a lot of essay and exposition, and I could just as easily work in the epigram as a proper quote, but for me it's all about the "space between spaces." Victor Frankl wrote, "Between stimulus and response there is a space. In that space is our power to choose our response. In our response lies our freedom."

I never expected to find this quote at the beginning of this chapter. I am one who takes up arcane and obscure pilgrimages, often called to go where no one wants to go. In college spring break, I wanted to find the grave of Walker Percy, who is best known for *The Moviegoer* but I prefer *The Second Coming*. *Lost in the Cosmos* is a hoot. He introduced me to Kierkegaard and the idea of trying to find God as a serious thing. He was inspired by his father's book *Lanterns on the Levee,* about life in Mississippi. The words at the top of this chapter come from there, these are the closing words, and I am sure that there is something about this wayfarer (even early Christians were followers of "the way" or "on the way") that is akin to the wandering repose of the chaplain. Specifically, these words came from a rare bookstore in New Orleans, that and the Cross of San Damiano the pilgrimage's only relics. The words seared into my soul. Indeed, I am branded.

People are mesmerized by stories of adoption. Once you really isolate this theme in your thinking, it's all over the culture. Abandonment and reunion are the primary stuff of drama and destiny. This is the archetype of *Lone Wolf and Cub*. Characters that are fated to wander are often adopted, in part because they have related problems and questions to answer, but also because the adoption experience has the unexpected gift of allowing the self to think new thoughts and to move around without the burden of excessive attachment. Such a person could move between family systems and social groupings and act as a catalyst for change.

Adoption is reserved for the heroic. The transcendent. The tragic. The spiritual. The wanderer. The everyman. (Not the *ubermensch* but the everyman.)

Everyone who has been alive, roughly 107 billion of them, has had parents. Most of us know who they are. So there's some natural shock and horror about the smaller group imagined by the larger. What would that be like? How could you not know? What if everything you believed about your origin turned out to be a lie?

Adoption is resonant because we don't know where we come from. And maybe we sense there is more to the story than we know. We were not there at our beginning. Indeed, the amnesia is like trying to remember our birth and before. And yet, we find ourselves here. How? And why? Ancestry is only a paltry placeholder for the real existential question. That is, the adopted person has a head start over the other who thinks that their parents are the answer to everything. We may not know who we belong to, but we surely know to whom we don't.

I initially connected with Wakefield's hymn when I was in Trenton, serving the dying without much time for my own family or even my own grandmother nearing the end of her life. Why am I serving these people, and not my people?

This is the task of the itinerant, and this is one of the big tensions in Scripture. How are we to read the basic human predicament. Is it exile? Or God's promised communion? Is it Ishmael—the abandoned—or Isaac—the favored son? Is it Cain, who is condemned to wander, or is it Joseph who is sent with purpose and saves his brothers? Is it Cain as exile doomed to be homeless, or is it Moses who must deliver the people of Israel to the promised land?

Starkly, are we God's children? Does that even mean anything? This world is so broken. If we are God's children, have we been entrusted to the care of the innkeeper like in the good Samaritan? Or, have we been left in the wrong part of town, by our parent, and night is falling fast, and danger is everywhere? The Cain/Moses dichotomy is as much the human condition as the liar riddle; they are one and the same.

How does the itinerant "lean in" to loneliness? Something about that loneliness looks radical and scary, like when Jesus threatens to come between father and son, and brother and brother. We don't want to lose family. For many of us, the church is our dysfunctional family of choice. Dare we let go of everything and follow God? That it is only when you let go of the world of everything you think you know, that you open yourself up to the hope of reaching out for God. And even though ministry is going to involve people, and billions of them, and communities and community life, something about following that call is a radically lonely ascetic, because that's what it is to follow God before all else.

CHAPTER 8

The Good, the Bad, and the Ugly

> He therefore turned to mankind only with regret.
> His cathedral was enough for him.
> It was peopled with marble figures of kings,
> saints and bishops who at least did not laugh in his face
> and looked at him with only tranquility and benevolence.
> The other statues,
> those of monsters and demons,
> had no hatred for him—
> he resembled them too closely for that.
>
> VICTOR HUGO

26

"Ugly" is a funny word. In our binary thinking, it is the opposite of good because we are so superficial as to equate good and beautiful. Don't get me started on the beautiful—Lucifer was the beautiful "light bearer." Let's just stick with the good, the bad, and the ugly. In this construction, the ugly is a third thing. It is neither good nor bad. It is something different.

Something different is a perfect category to explore disability, and especially disability as a point of *entre* into an existential dialectic. My life does not fit into the boxes. Having wrestled with the language, I'll reintroduce the term "marginalized." There are lots of people with marginalized perspectives because very few if any achieve the Platonic ideal. Many people don't fit in. Many people know they are different from the good, the beautiful, or the powerful. Many people experience the complexity of moving between complicated spaces.

I lived a different life. Shrug.

And while this life probably was not like yours, there are other people with physical disabilities. And I can say more about this too, and the way physical disabilities are hidden in our society. It's so statistically scarce, and so intentionally hidden, I wouldn't call it a community. But there are some kids that have things in common with other kids. And they will ride the school bus together.

At the same time, though, as I grew up with those other kids, there were things that made me very different from them. I was mainstreamed in my classes, and they were not. Mainstreamed means I got to take regular classes, and even advanced classes. And I had to fit in as best as I could with the regular kids. And for most of my life how I understood myself and my experience was having a foot in two worlds.

The "short bus" is my bridge term to convey to you the experience of two worlds. But it fails to describe how otherworldly disability is. I can share a few stark facts. I crawled on the floor until my surgery at thirteen. So while me and the other boys were worried about girls, I was worried they would see me crawl. In middle school I never left my desk or wheelchair for that reason.

I can tell you I never see disabled people, we are that few. I see lots of injured people, aged people, and obese people, but no one I would ride the short bus with. I fight over parking spaces with them and not one brings a wheelchair. I have worked for thirty years without a coworker in a wheelchair, in institutions with thousands of employees.

I frighten children to this day, pointed at from a hundred feet. It's painful on all sides. The children are frightened and it's sad to watch the parents hit their children because of me, as the parents flash through the oddity of shame and guilt at the sight of the natural. I wince from the future pain; thanks for the indelible negative association, Mom. That's going to improve the lives of many disabled people. Am I so hideous, woman, that like the Gorgon, if your child stares too long they will be reduced to stone and rubble? Of course, this is not what the mother intends, but of course this is what the child hears.

I would add that I can sort this out now, but try being the child who causes other children to be hit just by showing up. To be the child that causes other children to be hit, simply by entering a public arena. To wield such unspeakable magic. You have hit your child, mother, but I am bruised. It is a different life.

Lots of people have lived with a fear of a hidden secret. I am different in that too. I am not afraid of being found out. I am found every time, like searchlights in the prison yard. Like a thief apprehended by the light of the moon.

There is a peculiar kind of notoriety that comes with this. I have little sense of anonymity. Because there are so few of us in the professional sphere, I am remembered. People remember me. Cashiers remember me. Toll workers remember me. All of the random people that one interacts with—I am not random to them. I am "that guy." Often people remember my name; so I am careful to withhold it. This is not affected mystique. It's just really embarrassing to have every near stranger know your name, and you are lucky if you can recall the context where you saw their face. I call it "the celebrity of the grotesque." I have written of this elsewhere.

There is this thing happening in the academy that I do not like. In another book, I describe the academy as the Church of Reason, and it too suffers from its own dualistic dogma. After having found every kind of marginalized group there is, the Church of Reason has run out of categories to divide people by; it has run out of margins. So the latest fad is "disability theory" and these ideas win the day—for just a day—and then its on to the next fleeting idea. I probably won't get this published while disability is still "relevant," and that being the criterion of orthodoxy in the Church of Reason.

But even seventy-five years ago, there was no disability literature, and certainly not a hundred years ago. If there was a category, the category was suffering. And unless you suddenly die in a very sudden way, suffering will happen to you according to the Buddha. His information may be dated but I'm willing to risk it. The horror, then, is that sooner or later everyone will fall into it, only to be eclipsed by the larger group of the dead (and this is exactly why I do, and should, frighten children). I am not in a special interest group. I prefer the "authenticity" of frightened children who point for fear that this could happen to them, over the feigned respect of those who think I come from some exotic culture. Next to the dead, who at least are not obnoxious about it, I am in the largest group of all. And I got there before you. What does the book say? The last shall be first, and the first shall be last?

Years later after the short bus, stumbling through the seminary stacks, I found proof of Kierkegaard's disability. From his diary I read, "I . . . have been nailed fast to some suffering close to attend insanity the deeper cause of which must have had its roots in some disproportion between my soul and my body; it has no relation to my mind and spirit, on the contrary, and perhaps of the tense relationship between my soul and my body, have acquired a tensile strength rarely seen." My thought was: "Of course he knows what it's like, that's why his writing makes so much sense." Kierkegaard had many subjects. He initiated me into much of my thinking today, his school the mystery school of maieutic midwifery, orthodoxy, and—from first to last—dialectics. Dialectics are the most important—and most hidden—part of the liberal arts education. And with his dialectics, Kierkegaard taught me Socrates and Jesus and the importance of imaginative theology. His thought opened the parables and indirect communication. I was *his reader* and, as such, most of his books were dedicated to me. He changed my life and sent me on my quest in 1992 with *Fear and Trembling* (which he lovingly gives the subtitle *A Dialectical Lyric*) and he stamped my thinking on dialectics as if he were some Abelard with his masterpiece *Either/Or*.

(Can you see it even there? "Either" *this* "or" *that* itself is a dialectic frame where the two subjunctive possibilities are cast forever in dialectical tension. The book begins as a fiction within a fiction within a fiction. A fictional editor has found papers between two authors, and presents them to the reader in two groups. And we are left to weigh what is presented.)

27

Alienation is a common solution to difference, estrangement, and abandonment. With childish logic, the individual thinks, "Before you can reject me, I will alienate myself. Thank you very much, I'm leaving." My adolescence was buoyed from drowning by Pink Floyd's *The Wall*. Of course, this album was inspired by the problem of alienation and the desire to overcome it. But it was close enough and any lifeline will do.

One absolutely cannot overcome a problem by racing to self-inflict it before anyone else. Walls and bars are highly problematic coping strategies. I know it was Kaine, but I hear it as the paternal Master Po, "Grasshopper... Do the bars you have made keep the others out, or only cage yourself in?" Bars and cages have no use in solving the problems of freedom.

So, if the disabled experience is one of the many gateways to the marginal perspective, what is the vantage point from there? What does being different illuminate about the black and white?

You can say these abstract things like, "Dualism is the fall," or that "society is currently polarized" in a destructive way through social dualism. There are some buzzwords there; we hear a lot about polarization. But do we realize how destructive it is? Can you remember before 9/11? We were led to think that the ugly divide was between the American West and the Middle East. Have you seen exactly how acrimonious things have become in our own country between the Left and the Right since Bush?

We can say that dualism makes war possible, because it creates divisions of us and them. Read differently, dualism makes racism possible. Or sexism. Or anything. These are macro manifestations of the fractal inferences of dualism on the soul. This is what dualism does to the system as a whole. This is how dualism corrupts the collective unconscious. This is what dualism does to the world as a whole. We can agree that these things are problematic. We can write academic papers about what this means. The history of the world can be told, and even should be told, as the history of dualism and dialectic. Through dialectical philosophy, Hegel and Marx have a lot more insight on the violence of the century than do Lenin and Mao.

Dualism makes it possible to control the masses.

Great. But it's incredibly difficult to understand because we are so much in it. Such a work is like a school of fish putting together a treatise on water. As fish, we cannot really experience ourselves sufficiently out of the water to really, objectively understand the subject. Let's look at micro manifestations of the fractal inferences of dualism on the soul. You could say that the following are examples of the impact of dualism on individual psychology and spirituality.

Dualism creates unresolved grief and complicated grief. This comes up a lot in chaplaincy. Sometimes a patient has a difficult loss or life-change and before they think and feel all of the things that go with that loss or life-change, they encounter another big loss or life-change. Before the patient has completed the journey of one loss, another is demanded. Two or more losses too close together can result in a painful congestion of the soul. The congestion itself will clog and swell. All emotional work can get mired in the congestion and having any emotion at all can become too painful. At this point, patients no longer remember their original two or more losses, and they just focus on managing their feelings, which is nearly impossible because people are built to feel things that are meaningful; it's simply what we are. Not being what we are, not feeling what we must feel is the painful pathology at the root of much addiction. The addiction carries the false allure to allow the individual to ignore what they are feeling.

This even plagues students. Because of what we are and how we are made, people are basically a "one-thing-at-a-time" kind of creation. We can leverage the margins and make creative use of both hands at once, but really we are one-thing-a-time beings and when you really push that, the bandwidth starts to break down. This comes up all the time with beginning chaplains. They find themselves trying to "think" of the right things to say and do in the patient room, to remember their next verbatim, and to be self-aware of what they are doing. Meanwhile, they are having all kinds of feelings and emotions about what they are seeing, hearing, and remembering.

Consequently, the situation demands that they think and feel at the same time to do either very well, and this needs and benefits from much practice.

Dualism creates unthinkable thoughts and guilt. If this is clearly Good and that's clearly Evil, and there's no in-between, what am I to do with the parts of myself that aren't Good? I want to be Good, I want to be counted with those that are Good—I certainly don't want to be numbered among the Evil. But I can't really say that all of me aligns with the Good. So, the options that are left to me are not ideal. I can punish myself, I can try to banish these parts of myself. As a chaplain, I have to say that a lot of people lie when confronted with this; they lie to their communities, they lie to themselves, and they lie to God. These are all bad roads and places you don't want to go. Most people try to assuage this impossibility of the perfect Good by doubling down on their hatred of Evil and its projection elsewhere.

Dualism can fracture identity. I will say this elsewhere: this is how you split the soul. This is best illustrated by the complex divisions between the political Left and Right. Both of these extremes have positional platforms; that is, there is a cluster of aligned positions and my prefabricated identity is supposed to contain all of the prescribed opinions. If I have this value, then I am supposed to have these other values that are a part of the same platform. If I recycle, I'm supposed to have all of the Left opinions. If I have a gun, I'm supposed to have all the Right opinions. What if I like to use my recycling for target practice? Identity fractures each and every time one poor soul cannot harmonize all these cacophonous positions. It's very uncomfortable, and most people would do anything to avoid this feeling of fractured identity. On the macro scale, this is a form of control over the individual. This is how masks become politicized in the incredible midst of a global pandemic.

Said differently, dualism is the atomic force that can split the soul.

Dualism creates the sense that I can be absent from God. We get glimpses of this with Adam and Eve. Can we really hide from God? If I am enjoying something for myself, does that mean God is here blessing me? Such was not so for David in his iniquity. Or if I am enduring something so intense that I would rather choose not, does that mean God is not here? Is God only in the blessing? Is God the Almighty banned or barred from the tight place? If one man hates his menial job, and another loves it, is that job a blessing or curse? If a woman hates her body and another loves her body, is the body of a woman a blessing or a curse? Is it not the same job? Are not bodies basically the same? If God is only in the place I love, how can God ever lead me through the valley of the shadow?

Dualism opens the door to hatred. The dangers here are self-evident. Once I open the door to hatred, I might lose myself in it. Hatred and love are strong passions, and in extreme intensity they can be hard to distinguish. And if God is love, woe to the one who knows only hate.

Dualism can create a barrier in my spiritual life. Often this is couched in the conversation, "Why bad things happen to good people." Even Jesus rejects the moniker of being Good so this is already tricky. The conversation might be better titled, "Why bad things happen to those that are not so bad," but let's go forward. Someone says, "A Good God would not have allowed this Evil thing to happen to me fifteen years ago." This person, by their own admission, has been functionally stuck for fifteen years. For fifteen years their eternal conversation with God has been silent. One may be tempted to turn this into an abstract and academic question, but so long as they do nothing changes. At the end of the day their heart is broken and they don't know how to trust God again. How do you love—anyone—again after betrayal? This is an eternal conversation in need of a jump start, because fifteen years is just the first part of eternity. As a side note, a person with a disability is guaranteed a decade or two with this question. Everything you have ever loved is a blessing from God. Every blessing is a loan and you can't take any of them with you. When the term on the loan comes, is the God who granted it to be cursed? That seems a strange kind of banking with demonic reverse usury.

I can worship dualism and think that I can be worshipping God. This danger is expressed in the Genesis narrative. Is the act of trying to understand the difference between right and wrong really tantamount to the fall of humanity? You wouldn't think so. God wants us to do what's right, right? Isn't it important to know who are the white hats and who are the black hats? Isn't it important for me to know what to love and what to hate? These questions are very human, and they contain very human shadows. If I know for myself, do I need to trust God anymore? Do I need God for anything? Does the Knowledge of Good and Evil put me among the most intelligent in the universe? Can I serve Good and hate Evil, and have absolutely no relationship with God? Is it possible to be so completely focused on the difference between Good and Evil that I have essentially forgotten God, on my one-man crusade against everything I think I am supposed to hate, and God is reduced to an afterthought at best? Dualism is not God. The Bible is not God. My thoughts and ideas about God are not God. All these can be a part of a very subtle idolatry.

28

There is a reason why disability and the grotesque belong to the shamanic archetype. The shaman is the one who has to travel between worlds: the world of the divine, and the world of the mundane.

I have been extremely curious about this archetype for obvious reasons. Typically, beautiful women have a polarized reaction to me. They either hurry up and tell me everything, projecting safety. Or they run away entirely, anticipating loneliness. Neither is particularly true, although they can find safety under this traveler's cloak, and not under the mask of disability.

The archetype of the shaman is bountifully scattered across the sheer horror and brutality of the twentieth century, so it was easy to trace relative to my own location. It gets its start the previous century with Victor Hugo and *The Hunchback of Notre Dame*. It then repeats throughout the twentieth. It is *Phantom of the Opera*, as book, film, and musical, reiterated every thirty years or so. It is play and musical, theater and Disney. Think *Beauty and the Beast*, and every derivative thereof.

One of my favorite versions is especially American and modernist. *King Kong*. To me, the original film echoes so loudly of Joseph Conrad and *Apocalypse Now* thereafter. The black-and-white film has its own epigram to "Beauty and the Beast." Its savageness and horror, too, has been recycled every thirty years, with remake after remake.

The most archetypical expression of this came to me by the genius of Thomas Oden, who thought it might be useful for clergy to know the ancient myths. If we call it "The Beauty and the Beast," it finds its fullest expression with Vulcan and Venus.

Vulcan is born ugly, and cast off Olympus. That means, thrown away at birth, and like a meteor through the atmosphere, he hit the bottom of the ocean so hard he was disabled, and never after walked right. But, the ugly are clever because they can't get by on their good looks. The ugly and the weak have the gift of guile. Vulcan discovers the secrets of fire, like a broken Prometheus. He becomes a blacksmith because fire changes things and has great power (and the lame are always fascinated by power), and he conspires a plan to run off with the prettiest girl in the school, Venus. And it works! But eventually Venus becomes unhappy, because even with Venus, Vulcan is bitter. There's some irony here that the Vulcan in me smirks at. She runs off for a better life with the sexy god manly Mars. Mars is the god of war. Good luck with that.

There is more than one grain of truth in the Greek myth. There is something about the ugly that is granted access to the beautiful. It runs parallel to the eunuch and the priest, which somewhere hints that there is safety in celibacy. That is only if the celibacy is embraced, otherwise you're stumbling on broken anger and that's not safe at all. The ineffable and unspoken logic says that if this person has transcended the mesmerism of the male and female with all their conjugations and permutations, then this person has indeed transcended the human condition. With such control he then can now till the sacred soil and practice botany somewhere above the garden of Eden.

Eros is the child of Venus, so this might possibly be the ideal space to say that people are fascinated by the sexuality of the disabled. People have asked me about my fertility within minutes of meeting me. Other times, people work up to it and build up their gumption before they ask what they really want to ask. The Amazon driver was amazed that I could impregnate my wife. "But how did you?"—"Well, I could show you, but not from here." Why is my rejoinder any less appropriate than her gauche question? People often assume that my wife is my caretaker, and address her as if I were a pet or ward.

For the record, I'm not asexual, which is a peculiar projection of celibacy people have toward the disabled. This disclosure is not me expressing my sexuality at the reader. My confession is that my experience has been flooded by projections about my own sexuality by passersby. Sometimes women will approach me quickly and immediately expecting a celibate space and I can be unsettled by that—often they have a Catholic context. I can still awkwardly blush and become very nervous from the attention of beauty. But I know how to care about a woman and support her without making that erotic. I don't need to imagine myself as the focus of her erotic energy to see myself whole. I can want things for her that are good and that don't refer back to me. I don't need her to need me, in the way that perception and thinking becomes deceptively distorted ("She said that because she likes me, right?"). I have sat long enough among the ugly to have developed patience and altruism. If you can fully accept what will never be yours and still smile and marvel, you may find surprise that acceptance itself is more seductive than strength or brawn.

The strangest projection that people have toward the disabled is not regarding my sexuality. People have very rigid beliefs about my station in life, about my class and what I should or should not have. There are no limits to this: my fertility, my career, my income. When I worked through seminary at the university library, my classmates and co-workers continually complained to me that my use of the handicapped parking was a problem for them. You read that right: these are seminarians, whining and moaning about the injustice of my parking. But these reactions are common across the public. I guess they assume that their station ought be higher than mine and they have all kinds of ideas about what I have, about what I have achieved, and whether such is mine or theirs. They worry about what little I have without any appreciation of what it cost me. Sometimes people become enraged about what I have, and if they cannot take it they will try to destroy it. My life is fraught with blockade after barrier, but these malicious obstacles are the most cumbersome of all.

There is something wonderfully dialectical about Victor Hugo's treatment of the archetype. The hunchback is named Quasimodo, from the Latin meaning "halfway." Dialectic is about the tension and juxtaposition of two oppositional ideals. To describe his monster, Hugo places the guy somewhere in the middle, between ugly and beautiful, between human and inhuman. But for the life of me I can't imagine a better place to be.

CHAPTER 9

The Letters

> God speaks to each of us as he makes us,
> then walks with us silently out of the night.
> These are the words we dimly hear:
> You, sent out beyond your recall,
> go to the limits of your longing.
> Embody Me.
> Flare up like a flame
> and make big shadows I can move in.
> Let everything happen to you: beauty and terror.
> Just keep going.
> No feeling is final.
> Don't let yourself lose Me.
> Nearby is the country they call life.
> You will know it by its seriousness.
> Give Me your hand.
>
> RAINER MARIA RILKE

29

These letters are addressed to a young chaplain. Such a chaplain might be an intern in a CPE program, perhaps a seminary student in the summer. Or the chaplain may be a seasoned pastor who is exploring chaplaincy for the first time. The reason is that in this endeavor, both of these chaplains have more in common than they could possibly know. The intern CPE chaplain is maybe awash with feelings of inadequacy. "The reason for my distress is that I am too young. I have not been through anything, and everyone knows this by looking at me and my silly badge." The seasoned pastor is in a much worse plight: "I have done plenty of hospital visits in my day. I have lots of experience. Surely this can't be out of my reach." The reality is that both of these chaplains must go on a journey and become something new if they are to have any hope of reaching their destination.

I write these words with some heartache. I wonder how you might find these words, and how these words might find you. Kierkegaard begins his *magnum opus Either/Or* with the fiction that he found some letters, which he has been able to sort into two groups. He presents them as twice found. First they are found by a fictional editor (who is Kierkegaard), alleging that they were authored by two other authors (also Kierkegaard). They are responses to each other; at least they present opposite points of view. Finally, the whole project is presumably found by the reader. We will have more to say on things that are found later. This is the Dane's ruse, but how am I going to reach you who read these pages?

These "chaplains"—these characters—are not real people. They are hypothetical polarities representing points of view on a continuum. You who read this, however, are very much a real person. A heart beats within you, full of hopes, dreams, and desires known only to you and the God from whom no secrets are hid.

If we are to be honest, we have a lot of fear the first time we go into a patient room. Some of this is very, very human. Like a first kiss, if it's not a little scary when you go for it, you probably shouldn't bother.

And yet, something about the fear is holy. After all, this is ministry, out in the open, before God and everyone else, maybe like David and the ark.

30

And yet, something about the fear is unholy.

What if I get thrown out?

This is the first of three humiliations. It can be humiliating to be thrown out of a room; although, that can be a badge of courage. It is certainly humiliating to discover that one is self-absorbed when trying to do chaplaincy. Here I am trying to help someone on the worst day of their life, and I'm preoccupied with me. That's embarrassing.

Every person will have their own experience of acceptance and rejection. For those of us who have struggled with rejection, we must meet it once more as we begin this work.

There is comfort in the fact that most rejection of chaplaincy occurs because of the patient's religious transference toward clergy. It's not about you. And eventually that sinks in. How could they dislike me? They haven't met me yet.

But this solace blocks us from the greater gift. Rejection is a blessing.

Why is rejection a blessing? Because each person has their "yes," and each person has their "no." Each rejection is a confirmation of this. If there were no rejection, there would be no freedom. If there were no freedom, there would be no relationship. Relationship is the point.

Let me say this a little more explicitly. You might tell yourself that the worst possible outcome is getting rejected. That's simply not true. But if every patient reacted with, "I accept you, Chaplain, and I'm so happy to see you," that would not be a response. That would be a reaction. We do not have meaningful relationships with light switches. We walk in a room, turn the switch, and the lights come on. The light switch is a thing that we manipulate because it's an object and the object does what objects do. The light that follows is a reaction to the switch being operated. If the patients did this, each and every time with the predictability of a light switch, it would not be a relationship worth having. The occurrence of a "no" means that a true "yes" is possible, and that is a blessing. It could not be any other way.

31

What if I hurt the patient?

This is the second humiliation. These people are in pitiful shape and that all happened without you. It masks as an unrealistic sense of one's own importance. All patients are terminal. Of what are you really afraid?

This humiliation actually hides a fear of power. Sometimes you hear hyperbolic excuses. "I don't want to cut somebody open, and leave a wound that I don't have time to close." And adages like, "Don't open anything you can't close," and, "do no harm." Really? This is not surgery. This is someone who wants to tell you about their unanswered prayer. And if they don't want to talk about it, they'll tell me and change the subject. Each has their yes and no, and consent is negotiated at every point—every exchange—in the dialogue.

I don't cut my patients open. They come to me bleeding, bleeding on the floor, and the baby is crowning. Harm does not mean what you think it does when someone is birthing. Blood is normal.

If they are telling me something profound within ten minutes of saying "hello," which is more likely: that I am a special person with the power to cut people, or that this person has likely been trying for decades to get help from the first clergy who will listen?

32

What if I don't know what to say?

Congratulations. You have found the greatest fear and the greatest of the three humiliations. You are in good company, because the disciples were worried about the same thing. It is the greatest humiliation because through it one encounters true powerlessness. Through this humiliation we all become Job, we all become David, and we are all left crucified naked, and our only hope is elsewhere.

Simply put, someone's spiritual distress isn't something for me to do, in terms of me being prepared with some kind of textbook answer. That's really between them and God. What I can do is help with focus, and there.

33

When you enter the room, be as fearless as you can be, which means be as open as possible. Embrace whatever sad story may come and ask for more. The reason for this is that the first terrible thing is usually a test. They share the real tragedy if you do okay with the first one. People share things if they believe you want it. No one is going to let you hold the dead baby if they think you're going to drop it.

Even if you are frightened, want to not be. Even if you don't want the truth, want to want it. You will discover fears you never knew were yours. This is how the chaplain's confession works: it's inverted. By hearing the stories from outside, the darkness is found within. You want it darker.

34

After you have entered the room, gotten yourself past the hello and past the threshold to the physical space, a new question is born, "What separates me from the patient?"

There are practical considerations always about one's physical person. Do I stand or sit? Where do I put myself? And while one is thinking about the patient, one is also thinking about the door. With psych patients it's,

"What's between me and the door?" And with the medically sick, that question remains important. Stand too close to the door, and the patient will usher you out before you know it.

But this is different. It is not, "What do I do with me?" It is a more contemplative "What is between me and the patient?"

On a physical level this is really answered in a matter of feet. Although physicality can trigger attraction or revulsion, which also cast a footprint in the room.

On a very practical level, the answer to the question is transference and countertransference. There are things that the patient transfers onto the chaplain, and there are things that the chaplain counter-transfers onto the patient. This is where personal demographics come into play. Matters of race, gender, orientation, age, culture, education, language. Everybody has a piece of that. It cuts both ways. There are also the transferences and countertransferences that are unique to clergy, religion, and church. And although the terms are very useful, I'm sad to see so much academic psychology become so intrinsic to the care of the soul. I wish we had developed our own language.

There is another level even still. "What—precisely—lies between this soul and mine?" This is the beginning of contemplation.

This is also the first space of interest to the chaplain. Everything that can happen between the patient and chaplain is predicated by the various levels of this question.

35

There are two spaces of interest to the chaplain. The first important space is the space between the patient and the chaplain. But there is another space that is divinely important. The second space is the space between the patient and God.

A lot of criticism against what I'm saying is defensive in spirit. People don't want there to be a space between the patient and God for many reasons. Maybe they don't like the idea that there is a God. Maybe they don't like these kinds of declarations because what they want is to keep their functioning blurry and undefined. I'm inviting a certain kind of consciousness in the work; and Freud said the greatest of all desires is to remain unconscious, and as surely as chaplains are clergy they are not above desire. Or even though a particular chaplain claims that there is a God, they have learned to carry their chaplaincy in such a way that they would never want to assume that the patient would say that there is a God. That is, they deny themselves a model of faith-based chaplaincy because the patient may not have faith. This seems like an unnecessary contortion to me, but in this book of confessions, it happens.

So, let it be said that is the space between the patient and God, and it is known by many names. This is known as the patient's spirituality. This is also known as the patient's spiritual life. Sometimes it's called a spiritual practice. In my training, I call it "the Dominant Response to God" because it has a dialogical context, content, and purpose. It is quite likely that the patient has a different understanding about the nature of God than I do. I can't find two or three Methodists that I agree with, so I don't know why I would expect some random patient to see the world the way I do. Even an atheist has a philosophy of life. Even an atheist has an idea of what it means to be alive.

One final disclaimer. It is important to respect that the patient's spiritual life has long preceded the relationship with the chaplain. God has been working in this person's life long before I showed up, and I'm in no race to discredit that. I met a man that God rescued from the Holocaust, and I'm not about to dishonor their relationship just because he won't pronounce the Tetragrammaton and I will.

These two in-between spaces create a new space where the chaplaincy actually happens. On one side is that which is between the chaplain and the patient, the chaplain-patient space. On the other side is that which is between the patient and God, the God-patient space. In between those two hyphenated spaces is chaplaincy. That is the area of professional concern and clinical focus. Chaplaincy is between the chaplain-patient space and the God-patient space. There are three persons in every visit: God, the chaplain, and the patient. There are three spaces in every visit: the chaplain-patient space, the God-patient space, and the chaplaincy space. Although the patient is in all three spaces, resist the urge to think of it as a chaplain-patient-God space. That invites confusions and unnecessary clouds. All three persons are not the same, and they have specific roles.

36

Nothing can really happen to the chaplain.

This can be a funny discovery. For all of the surrounding fear and trembling, it's pretty clear that the chaplain is going to walk out of the room just fine, and many patients don't. Maybe the chaplain will get disrespected, but that's hardly an occupational hazard when you look at suffering in the face.

The room is a place of safety. It is a place of connection. It's comforting to think of the room as a sanctuary. It is the space where the priest is at home, free to preside and worship at will. It is where I experience the sacrament, and consecrate it. Such a sanctuary is not a stage, but it is an arena where one lives and moves, and knows completely perhaps even to the point where boundaries between self and sanctuary have completely dissolved. Just by being in the room, the chaplain can trust that everything that needs to happen will happen. The room is where you have everything you need.

For this reason, it is always the chaplain who decides when the visit begins and ends. Even if the patient tries to kick out the chaplain, the chaplain remains accountable to God as to what happens next.

Of course, some things will happen to the chaplain. The chaplain has to witness all this, and if good questions arise, the chaplain will take them home. So, on one hand it is completely true: the chaplain is perfectly safe. On the other hand, the chaplain will be changed. That's what dialogue does. If you witness enough suffering you're not going to be the same guy. But if you don't want to change, don't get in a conversation with God.

37

We've been obsessing about the room. Our anxiety has made it a binary thing: either in the room, or out of the room. We have been out of the room, and our whole hope has been to make it into the room. Out of the room, we have been spiraling in shame and guilt, and doing so has not made it any easier to get into the room. Perhaps we have spent significant time bowing at the altar of self-loathing. Idolatry does not make going into the room any easier, either.

Now that we are actually in the room, we find that the room itself was only a door. It was a door to three persons and three places. And in the vaulted place of chaplaincy itself one can see signs and wonders.

38

My own ministry has been marked by another room, and it is much like the patient room. In fact, I exchanged one room for the other without noticing because the rooms are so similar. I'm describing the room of supervision. The room of supervision also has three persons, and three places. But there is also a window overlooking the patient room.

I think of supervision as a direct parallel to what the chaplain intern is doing. The supervisor has more concerns and manages a different relationship to the hospital, and to the patient, than the intern does. But the core accountability is to God. There is this concept in clinical supervision that enumerates a "clinical rhombus." It's a fixture in supervision theory. It creates meaningful parallels in a constellation between the chaplain, patient, supervisor, and larger institution. That larger institution is important. I get that. The larger institution is the vested party that provides the material resources that make the chaplaincy. But I don't like models for ministry that don't include God. You can squeeze God into the rhombus, but that just feels wrong. What is it then, a pentagram? I think I'll stick with my party of three. I think the sacredness of the encounter demands that the expression have the fewest terms, not the most.

39

There is one more room I have not mentioned. It has been hidden; a room within a room. The thing about these hidden rooms is that they are often left unexplored, and the main reason why people don't even look for them is because they think they are there already. Many times a young chaplain will come full stop in the doorway thinking, "Well this is it; I've arrived at my destination and now we will see if my work is a success or failure," as if this were a trial run of the last judgment. They don't find the three persons, or the three places, because all awareness has literally been checked at the door.

But there is a hidden room. Perhaps what another text calls "darkness within darkness." Reach into the darkness and you can open the door.

It has some resonance with our discussion of the patient room. People have preconceived notions about the room. They have ideas and judgments about what the room means. They have fears about what they will find, and they have fears about finding themselves. They have an entire belief structure about what the patient room is and is not. And once they go inside, the real experience begins.

You may go there whenever you like. You may retreat to it whenever you wish. It is another place between persons. It is a place that requires that you reach for it, but rest assured it is within reach. Is the greatest capacity that we have as human beings.

The room within a room is a place where you can go and do the most important work there. You can explore the most terrible things. Like Adam, you can name things. You can bang on some clouds. You can name the monsters and the angels. *You can be honest.*

You can continue the only conversation that matters. It is the only conversation where you as a being actually make sense.

It is the place of prayer.

CHAPTER 10

The Chasm

> For meanwhile the tightrope walker had begun his performance:
> he had stepped out of a small door and was walking over the rope,
> stretched between two towers
> and suspended over the market place and the people.
> When he had reached the exact middle of his course
> the small door opened once more and a fellow in motley clothes,
> looking like a jester, jumped out and followed the first one with quick steps.
> "Forward, lamefoot!" he shouted in an awe-inspiring voice. . . .
> And with every word he came closer and closer;
> but when he was but one step behind, the dreadful thing happened
> which made every mouth dumb and every eye rigid:
> he uttered a devilish cry and jumped over the man who stood in his way.
> This man, however, seeing his rival win,
> lost his head and the rope, tossed away his pole,
> and plunged into the depth even faster, a whirlpool of arms and legs.
> After a while the shattered man recovered consciousness
> and saw Zarathustra kneeling beside him.
>
> NIETZSCHE

40

Zarathustra is a meaningful reference several times over. Nietzsche reintroduced Zarathustra to the world precisely because he is interested in the world beyond the dualism of Good and Evil. Nietzsche's primary project is very close to ours. He finds himself in the modern age wondering aloud about who and what we ought to become. In the story here, the jester is the "new man" leaping over yesterday's tightrope walker.

Zarathustra becomes a puppet of sorts for Nietzsche. It is carnival for sure, with this circus of tightrope walkers, jesters, and ventriloquists. Through the sage's mouth, Nietzsche is able to describe his own wisdom.

I, too, want to find a path beyond Good and Evil.

So Zarathustra becomes the German's artifice. Fine. But Zarathustra has his own rightful place in the conversation. He is all but unknown to us today, but he has been well known across the centuries. Mozart puts him in the "Magic Flute," and Handel also uses him as a character in opera. Zarathustra is also known in antiquity as Zoroaster, the philosopher and prophet of Zoroastrianism, known as the first great monotheistic religion in the Indo-Iranian consciousness. Zarathustra remains shrouded in eternal mystery. We don't even know when his dates were. Someone seems to be using his name between 500 and 600 BC, a very key time for him and thinkers like Anacharsis (and thus us), but the religion he founded seems to go back to 1300 or earlier.

Zoroastrianism itself is fascinating. It is renowned for introducing monotheism into the world with Ahura Mazda as the supreme being (yes, that Mazda) and Ahriman as the embodiment of evil. But these two are opposites, and this is the origin of the light side versus the dark side (and why chess was so compelling to the Persian consciousness—even a thousand years later when Islam entered into the world; it's entirely built into the game: "checkmate" means the sheik is dead). And suddenly, we realize that we are not talking about monotheism at all, but a rigid duality between Good and Evil. Zoroastrianism even has a story like Eden with an evil serpent (although this will come centuries later), as do the Babylonians (and this comes centuries prior).

None of this is lost on Nietzsche.

For what it's worth, I settled on the Nietzsche quote because I am a sucker for parables. I thought this was a great visual for the chapter on the chasm. As someone who is perpetually learning to walk, sentenced to forever take first steps, I resonate profoundly. I love the image of the walker, my own life having been a peculiar tightrope. I love the tightrope as an expression of dialectic and dualism, the two towers, and all that was undone in the era of 9/11. I love the humanity of the "whirlpool of legs," myself who has fallen too often, myself all too familiar with the urge to cast oneself into the abyss, and I feel the magnetism of the ground every time I see it, the *l'appel du vide*, French for "fear of the void" that is really more a fear of oneself and throwing oneself into it (I don't know why the French get to name all the good feelings).

When you realize how destructive dualism is, the question quickly emerges: where does it come from? The answer has as much to do with *l'appel du vide* and the chasm as it does the polarities we idolize.

41

The absolute stupidest thing I have ever heard about the origin of dualism is that it's the mother's heartbeat. This might be called the "cardio-social animal" theory of dualism. The idea is that because we hear the heartbeat in utero, we are "programmed" for binary thought. Meaning, because of the bombardment of sound, beat, rest, beat, rest, beat, rest, and so on, we thus think in extremes. Because we think in extremes, we see things as black and white. That's what they say, but you can't find one of them that says it.

This lies in the dangerous territory of beyond stupid. Think, for a moment, of how many creatures have hearts—and mothers. Is this to say that the entire animal kingdom is prone to dualism? Every single living thing that is born is a natural binary thinker? Forget about the humorous possibility of radical whales; is there any evidence of political extremism among primates? Extremists are a lot like monkeys in a zoo that throw their excrement at onlookers, but is there any evidence the other way around?

Or consider this: every new mother who can goes out and buys a Doppler so she can hear the baby's heartbeat. And it rings loud and clear. Wouldn't the baby, being of the same fluid atmosphere, be just as "programmed" by two heartbeats? Its own and the mother's? Or what about twins? Or mammals born in a litter? What about children born deaf? Does this mean that the deaf are spared from all extremist thinking and should be groomed and installed as public servants?

What if the notion were true? How do we fix that? How do we silence the womb? Or fill it with new sound, as to better "program" the thinking? Moreover, I'm not that smart. I meditated on this theory for about a minute. We are left with the question, "Why would anyone seriously suggest something so profoundly silly?" This kind of thinking is exemplary of "evolutionary psychology," which might be better termed "evolutionary mythology." What you do is you have some value that you want to espouse, and then you make up an evolutionary myth that supports your value or worldview.

In 1992, I traveled to Cambridge. Electric scooters were less popular there and then, and a plucky folk will ask questions about how it runs and works. I learned a lot. *I could say anything.* Anything. As long as I wrapped up with a remotely cohesive metaphor, almost any science fiction would do. I could say "petrol." There was no sound of a gas motor, and the fumes would mean death for indoor use, but they would take it. I could literally say "rubber bands" and present complicated mechanics of winding the reverse rubber bands while traversing forward. I'm not joking. I would say that the wheelchair ran on rubber bands and people believed it. People would believe it because the theory had complexity and it was green for the environment. My favorite was to say "nuclear" and then dismiss and discredit the dangers of radiation poisoning (while scratching myself).

What people need is a placeholder, and little more. The placeholder blocks the question, and the answer to the question would be telling. But the imposition of the placeholder creates questions of its own. Who introduced the placeholder, and why?

There is no greater placeholder than the presence of an answer—even a feeble or flimsy one. If I think I know why something is the way that it is, then I stop asking questions altogether. This is the trap of recognition. If I recognize something then I do not wonder what it means. If I know what something means to me, then I think I know what it means to everyone. And all curiosity disappears. If a life event was sad for me, I may fail to invite the patient to explore their own feelings about their own life event because I am deluded that their feelings are identical to mine and thus I already know what everything means.

The joke is that "You always find it in the last place you look!" This is a playful admonition to keep searching. Why would you look after you have found something? If you found your keys why would you keep looking for them? But when it comes to the search for meaning and motive we tend to stop once we hit on one of the seven deadly sins. "Oh, I know why they did this; it was for lust." Or, "They did it for the money." There are other possibilities. Such as a multitude of sins and total depravity. Indeed, you can find all of the seven deadly sins without exposing the desire to control others, which just might be the greatest of all sins. The desire to control others is, in fact, the composition of all seven.

42

I have said that dualism is the fall. Where does dualism come from?

This is extremely hard to answer. I can say something about the history of dualism. Dualism happened 539 to 486 BC.

My attention turned to Cyrus completely accidentally. I was working on a different question entirely. In the West, there is an opposition between

Heraclitus and Parmenides. Heraclitus writes about eternal change and Parmenides writes about eternal Oneness. In good conscience, I cannot write so much about Heraclitus and never cite his most famous quote: "You cannot cross the same river twice." Heraclitus is the patron philosopher of flux and change.

In the East, there is a parallel contrast between Lao Tzu and the Tao against Confucius and the Divine Order. Strangest of all, Heraclitus and Lao Tzu sound a lot like each other, to the point where if this was high school, somebody's getting in trouble for plagiarism.

Why? How? These thinkers are thousands of miles and cultures apart. How can they sound so similar? Like lightning, can Divine inspiration really strike twice? What are the odds? But it's this kind of awe that leads Karl Jaspers to call this the Axial Age, and say that the universe has some kind of special sauce of spiritual awakening that exists at this time and no other.

I am passionate about nondualism and both Heraclitus and Lao Tzu are beautiful writers of nondualism. And then it occurs to me. What if they are not so much like each other, but they are writing against the same thing? Indeed, the enemy of my enemy might well pass for my closest friend. And what were they writing against? The Achaemenid Empire of Cyrus the Great: the largest geopolitical force of dualism in the history of civilization until the United States. Cyrus's reign touched them both East and West, and at the same point in history.

I begin to spend time with Cyrus. Cyrus is a monster, and between the reign of Cyrus and Darius something monstrous happens.

Cyrus was a Zoroastrian, sort of. I've briefly mentioned Zarathustra and that religion. What I haven't said is that the Zoroastrian priests are called magi, and this is where we get the word "magic" from. Five hundred years later, a certain Christ child will be visited by three magi. These are the "wise men," or kings, from the nativity. I have always been curious about Jewish thought and monotheism, and how this becomes Christian thought and deciphering what the magi have to do with it.

What you get by pretending to be Zoroastrian is a religion of pious credibility. With their strong polarity of Good and Evil, Zoroastrians have theological beliefs about lies, similar to Christianity's posture toward lies in the garden of Eden. I say Cyrus was sort of Zoroastrian. When Zarathustra initiates his religion he criticizes the priests and magi of his day, not unlike any religious reformer. So Zoroastrianism is born out of this larger religious context of magi, magi who worship Mithra. If Cyrus believes in magi at all, it is surely these Mithraic priests. Mithraism is a dead religion, but centuries later it will have a lot of interaction with Christianity as a mystery religion and then again in forms of Christian gnosticism. Apologies to the reader;

the threads of cause and effect are interwoven and you can't describe these braids of meaning as a singular thread or timeline.

A dear friend of mine marked the Cyrus Cylinder to me, a large historical artifact that Cyrus commissioned as propaganda. I had no idea it was even there. It has a big chunk missing which I'm convinced contains the entire text of Shelley's "Ozymandias." I am thrilled and for an evening I feel like a swashbuckling archaeologist now having some connection between Heraclitus and the Tao. What seems strange is to think that Heraclitus/Parmenides and Lao Tzu/Confucius are happening in isolation. It makes more sense that they are responding to the polarized ethos that permeates the kingdom of Cyrus the Great. But it reveals just as much about how Cyrus does business. It establishes both Cyrus as the link and his *modus operandi* and cements his branding as "Cyrus the Benefactor." What he does is conquer a people, insert himself as the culmination of their religion, and forever weave himself into their historical narrative. The Cyrus Cylinder demonstrates and models this with the Babylonians. He says the god Marduk has favored him and appointed him to lead the conquered Babylonians. I would call it psychological warfare, but psycho-spiritual is a better term. What our politicians and priests of the military industrial complex call "the battle for hearts and minds."

This is, in fact, what Cyrus does with the Hebrews. He has a few religiously friendly political policies. The Second Temple is commissioned. Much of the Bible gets written down as the oral tradition goes on paper. Genesis is written and the stories of Abraham and the stories of Moses are woven together. The Jews are allowed to return to Jerusalem. Unbelievably, Cyrus gets himself written into the Scripture as the Messiah—the one and only long awaited Messiah. How does that even happen? Centuries later, my Messiah Jesus will say,

> "The kings of the Gentiles exercise lordship over them; and they that exercise authority upon them are called benefactors. But ye shall not be so: but he that is greatest among you, let him be as the younger; and he that is chief, as he that doth serve. For whether is greater, he that sitteth at meat, or he that serveth? is not he that sitteth at meat? but I am among you as he that serveth."

For Jesus, "benefactor" is an epithet.

Cyrus conquers the known world, with power and might, but I don't see how he can say he does this as a pious Zoroastrian. Remember, good Zoroastrians don't lie. He has blasphemed his own gods as well as Babylonian and Hebrew. Cyrus achieves this in about nine years. The weapon of psycho-spiritual warfare is unstoppable. This is between 539 and 530.

The only thing more devastating is what's to come: Darius. The karma and irony here on an atomic scale. In a mere eight years, Darius will be king, Cyrus beheaded, and his sons dead. And Darius will do it all in the name of Cyrus.

Everything about Darius is a lie. We call his empire the Achaemenid Empire only because Darius named it that. "Achaemenid" is a reference to a remote relative that loosely links Darius and Cyrus together. So Darius creates the brand that includes himself with Cyrus. It is anachronistic (by design) to use Achaemenid to refer to anything before Darius. And by the same token, it is deception (by design) to use Achaemenid to refer to anything after Darius. And, if you get to write the history, you really can get away with murder.

A lot of the story about Darius comes from Darius. He left behind a record meant to be his eternal PR. Most famous is the "Behistun Inscription." This is a pictograph and narrative, carved into a monolith as the world's first billboard of how Darius deposed the false king Gaumata and liberated the people and restored the house of Cyrus. It's all spin and fake news. Darius "Cyruses" Cyrus himself, weaving himself into the religion of Cyrus's self-worship in exactly the same way that Cyrus did this to other religions. Darius the Mede has learned the art of manipulating the media from Cyrus. Darius is now Messiah, and the pictograph is complete with the Zoroastrian logo, the *faravahar*, like a politician with an upside-down Bible photo op.

This brings me to an interesting question. What if "Darius the Mede" from the book of Daniel was actually "Darius the Great"? Daniel is arguably one of the five most important books in the whole thing. After all, Darius the Great was a Mede. Why is this such a stretch of the imagination?

This question doesn't get much traction because Belshazzar is referenced in the story, but the historical Belshazzar immediately precedes Cyrus—not Darius. So instead of throwing out one data point (the naming of Belshazzar), biblical historians scratch the whole text (which is a perfect description of Gaumata). Never mind if there's a simple error, or the kind of misdirection Darius has practiced so well. Never mind that Cyrus has gotten himself inserted in the text. Never mind that the shoe fits. Belshazzar is described as a usurper. That sounds like the Gaumata I know.

How many names does Gaumata have? Smerdis. Bardiya. Oropastes. Sphendadates. Tanoxares. Mergis. Mardos. Possibly Patizeithes (that could be Gaumata's brother). That's ten right there. I'm cheating a little bit because some of the multiplicity of names is directly due to language differences. But the point stands. Why not Belshazzar? It's pretty obvious the guy doesn't care what you call him. Multiple identities are not a problem for Gaumata, and one can only wonder who is the more talented Mr. Ripley, Darius or Gaumata.

I think Gaumata was in on it from the beginning. I think Darius needs a pathway to legitimacy. Darius has no right relation to Cyrus. So, he is the lance bearer of Cambyses (Cyrus's son and immediate successor), and Cambyses is convinced to kill his younger brother Bardiya (through dreams, gods, and omens). Gaumata is a look-alike for Bardiya and gets to be in charge for a while. Cambyses actually died from a freak horse mounting accident that goes gangrene (who's that lance bearer again?). Gaumata is the heir apparent. He has good poll numbers and the people love his tax policies. Darius comes in and kills the nine conspirators that Gaumata needed to complete the coup. And Darius is venerated for restoring the house of Cyrus. If Darius and Gaumata are working together, everybody wins. Or as Heraclitus says, "A hidden connection is stronger than one you can see."

The clincher for me is that Darius marries the daughter of the original Bardiya, so that his children can have lineage to Cyrus. The irony is pure evil. He didn't just kill both sons. He has to marry the granddaughter. The lineage of Cyrus is dead and Darius sleeps with his granddaughter. It's either pure hatred, pure obsession, or both.

After Gaumata is gone, Darius offers the court philosopher role to none other than Heraclitus. The only thing more unbelievable than that coincidence is that Heraclitus actually declines. Who dares defy Darius and lives? I'm not sure that Heraclitus is the exception. His own death was particularly gruesome, and his body is found in manure. I can't help but wonder if he was dead or alive when he goes into the pile.

The temptation is to think that the invitation into the court of Darius as evidence of the congruence in their thought. Remember, what put Cyrus on my radar at all is that Heraclitus and Lao Tzu are so unified in writing their nondualism, presumably against the dualistic reign of Cyrus-Darius. Darius may have completely betrayed Cyrus, but he's not changing the tune of the state radio; he's still on the faux-Zoroastrian station. Is it that Heraclitus and Darius are secret best friends, or is it that Darius is interested in further inserting dualism into the philosophy of his state-sponsored faux-Zoroastrianism? Heraclitus could be useful in a project like that. Moreover, the *Fragments* of Heraclitus are not particularly gracious to the magi or the initiates of the ancient mysteries, and this disdain only gets louder if we imagine that these words are written after Darius's offer, while taking refuge in the Temple of Artemis. No, what caught my eye in the first place is that Heraclitus is clearly a nondualist writing at a time when Darius is asserting this cultural religion of dualism (all the while, that religion *was* a religion of monotheism). Lao Tzu, the same. Clearly their projects align on nondualism, and clearly against the dualism of Darius.

If Gaumata is Belshazzar, the biblical writing on the wall is meant for him: "Thou art weighed in the balances, and art found wanting."

43

So, that's the genesis of dualism and that also might be the story of how the Tree of Dualism got in Genesis. But does that answer it? Does that tell us from where does dualism come?

There is certainly the geopolitical assertion of dualism that we find with Cyrus, but in order for that to have happened, all of the pieces had to be on the board already. Cyrus doesn't create dualism as much as he exploits it. Cyrus can shape the narratives into written texts, but those narratives had to be there to begin with. Cyrus can get himself named as the messiah, but there had to be the expectation of a messiah already.

You can look into the religion of Zoroastrianism; this only takes you into Indo-Iranian-Mesopotamian spirituality. Mithra becomes a key factor in the history here. Remember, the magi priests belong both to the Zoroastrians and Mithra worshippers. Mithra himself becomes a peacemaker between Ahuramazda (sometimes written as one word) and Angrimaynu. The lasting influence of Mithra should not be underestimated. He's a dead ringer for the Statue of Liberty. And if you want to understand the origins of the rites of the Christian church, don't look at Judaism. Look at Mithra. He's gotten into everything.

This is significant. It is hard to decipher, distinguish, and disentangle the religions of Mithra and Zarathustra, because that is what the Mithra magi wanted. They like to blur things. But there are a few undeniable facts. (1) Zarathustra was critical of the priestly class. (2) Zarathustra was killed by the priestly class. (3) Zarathustra does not like the priestly treatment of cows (you see the commonalities in the Indo-Iranian matrix). The great Mithra symbol always depicts Mithra slaughtering the bull. Over centuries, Zoroastrianism was reimagined as a vehicle for Mithra. But these are not the same religions.

In retrospect, it is easy to imagine that all of the magi from every period were in alignment with themselves. Not true. It is easy to imagine that the religions of Cyrus, Darius, and Zarathustra were the same. Or that all of the religions of the region were in alignment. Not true either. Darius went to extraordinary pains at Behistun to make you think so. But Cyrus was killed and beheaded by a woman, the mighty Tomyris. Whether he was a self-proclaimed Zoroastrian or a servant of the Mithraic order, he certainly wasn't in lockstep with Tomyris and the Massagetae people, a matriarchal culture. I half wonder if Heraclitus's decision to live the end of his life in the Temple of Artemis wasn't an attempt to take refuge in the same matriarchal culture, in the way our whistleblowers hide in embassies. After the beheading of Cyrus, even Darius would think twice about desecrating the Temple of Artemis.

One of the interesting details here is that Zarathustra (according to Zoroastrians) and Cyrus overlapped. That means in the very next generation following the prophet, Zoroastrianism was co-opted as a fake religion by Cyrus. That is, Cyrus was not a pious Zoroastrian that did something unique to Hebrew and Babylonian religion. You can add Zoroastrianism to the beginning of the list. Religious story is Cyrus's favorite weapon.

I don't think that Zarathustra was trying to create a dualism. I think he was trying to set Ahuramazda at the top of the heavens, with the forces of light and dark both underneath. But Zarathustra is killed in the lifetime of Cyrus, and Cyrus is already instrumental in his revision.

I write about these names, because these are the names that come up in trying to trace the origins of dualism. But that does not mean you've found the answer. Where else could you look?

You can try to trace the origins of monotheism. Akhenaten was an Egyptian monotheist that emphasized the sun, but it's hard to consider him the cultural source of monotheism because the religion reverted after him and there wasn't a legacy of generations. In Semitic thought, Abraham is considered the grandfather of monotheism. But looking at his life as the source of monotheism doesn't shed much light on dualism. One thing that does intrigue me about Abraham is he has an encounter with Melchizedek, who doesn't get much story in the text but he is essential in establishing the Christian priesthood. He comes from Ur (that's Iraq) and presumably a Sumerian context. Sumerian gods may appear in the Bible as the Anakim and others. There's a lot of overlap between Babylonian and Sumerian mythology. They have stories like Adam and Eve and the paradise of Eden, but again, the Tree of Dualism doesn't really appear until Cyrus.

So you can poke at these lost civilizations and ancient religions and never find the smoking gun as to who fired the bullet of dualism. You could say it was Adam and Eve, or even the rebellion of Lucifer, a light bearer like Mithra. It's fun to contrast the precession of the astrological ages with a very loose sequence of biblical tradition. The Zodiac runs from Leo, to Cancer, to Gemini, to Taurus, to Aries, to Pisces (the sign of Jonah). It's a period of about 2,156 years per zodiac sign. There are a few interesting observations. The Age of Taurus is marked by the sacrifice of bulls, perhaps a context for

Baal worship and even Mithra's slaying of the bull. That transitions to the sacrifice of rams, which is the sign of Aries. Looking at the zodiac might steer your thinking to Gemini (the twins) as the onset of dualism (think of all the stories about brothers in the Bible: Cain/Able, Isaac/Jacob, Isaac/Ishmael). But the wiser age to look at could be Cancer, which would be about ten thousand to eight thousand years ago. The zodiac is a reflection of our mythological development. We recognize the sign of cancer as a crab, but the earlier version was a double vortex that reminds me of the Taoist yin-yang. The double vortex is a meaningful contrast from the singularity of Leo whose mane is the sun; going from a monism to a dualism. But this is grabbing at anything.

The zodiac is old, although the only thing I have found older than ten thousand years is the Bonpo religion. This is a very dualistic religion of good and evil, and it comes from Tibet. The dates of origin are wildly conflicting. Some dates are as old as eighteen thousand years ago. And other dates suggest that the main prophet of Bon was in the court of Cyrus the Great. While this is hard to confirm, it is a fact that at some point, these Tibetans came into contact with Indo-Iranian thought and received the "Wheel of Mithra." ("The wheel in the sky keeps on turning—"? That wheel.) It's all over their art. We know this symbol as the swastika, and when Germany takes the swastika as its symbol, it receives the symbol back from Tibetan exploration and the Bonpo religion. I don't think the Bonpo would have ever embraced Mithra without being pre-programmed in the dualistic consciousness.

Where else can you look? Since dualism manifests in social and individual psychology, I can look to the academic tradition of psychoanalysis. For Freud the story of the other is the story of the self and mother. Harry Stack Sullivan will expound on this in his "object-relations theory." The nomenclature seems crass to me. There are certain things I don't want to "objectify" when it comes to understanding the soul, God, or dualism. And I want to give Sullivan a lot of credit because he spends a lot of thought considering what happens between persons, and what happens within a person, and even the meta question of what the one (intrapersonal) has to do with the other (interpersonal). But this is neither a smoking gun on the genesis of dualism, nor definitive about human nature.

At this point, I should disambiguate between Freud and the Freudians, and especially all of the academic Freudians of my field (which is chaplaincy no less) who have thoroughly convinced themselves that care of the soul is essentially psychotherapy. This is a great misunderstanding and consistent with the way that academic American Freudians especially are more fascinated with sex than Freud himself was. With a great lust, it is tempting to think that sex itself is the origin of dualism, that we have eroticized transcendence and confused transcendence with the mere difference between male and female. This is easy to do; sex is, by definition, engrossing. But just because you can locate dualism between genders, just like genitals are located between the legs, doesn't mean that's where dualism originates. Believe it or not, oh you lusty Freudians, there are things in this life that even precede sex. One of my favorite Zen masters, Tesshu Yamaoka—master of the "no-sword" technique—spent years misunderstanding the man/woman problem by pursuing sex as a means of transcendence. After many, many hours of conjugating through concubines, his wife could stand no more and he realized it was a dead end. Several things about this episode make me snicker. Even the mighty Zen masters are beguiled into thinking sex is inherently transcendent.

But teasing out Freud from the Freudians only gets us so far. If psychoanalysis can only, once again, blame the mother, are we really any better off than we were with the ridiculous "socio-cardio" theory? I ask myself this all the time: are we really getting anywhere? Theologian Martin Buber is keenly aware of the tendency to confuse the great Thou of life with the mother-baby relationship. He writes:

> The prenatal life of the child is a pure natural association, a flowing toward each other, a bodily reciprocity; and the life horizon of the developing being appears uniquely inscribed, and yet also not inscribed, in that of the being that carries it; for the womb in which it dwells is not solely that of the human mother. This association is so cosmic that it seems like the imperfect deciphering of a primeval inscription when we are told in the language of Jewish myth that in his mother's womb man knows the universe and forgets it at birth. And as the secret image of a wish, this association remains to us. But this longing ought not to be taken for a craving to go back, as those suppose who consider the spirit, which they confound with their own intellect, a parasite of nature. For the spirit is nature's blossom, albeit exposed to many diseases. What this longing aims for is the cosmic association of the being that has burst into spirit with its true You.

Buber says no. This is not about our encounter of the mother. There is something bigger here. This is about our encounter with the Creator. If we are created for relationship with God, and God is going to be veiled from us, this is going to be for each of us the proverbial splinter in the mind, perhaps because our very souls are splintered. Perhaps the great chasm is our experience of being the creation, ever longing for Creator.

In order for dualism to be what it is; that is, this thing that gets imagined and interpreted into everything, it would have to be pretty close to the base level of reality. It is like a fractal that shows up microscopically and written large against the vastness of the cosmos.

And it is. Dualism is a function of the fact that we are created, and because this fact precedes every other detail of our existence, it is then very easy to turn dualism—in all of its forms—into a god.

I have often wondered if this is why the story of dualism is presented in such an engendered way. When you say that men can do this because they are men and women can do that because they are women, and absolutely nothing can happen that blurs the lines, we then accept the gender dualisms and all that goes with because sex is very close to base reality. That is, we all wake up in this world and find ourselves to be engendered in some configuration or other. And when the text names this as a foundational fact we accept it as sacred without question.

Let me say this again. If people can be so easily and frequently fooled into believing that worshipping dualism is the same thing as worshipping God, it must resonate on a very similar frequency to our core spiritual estrangement in life. The chasm between us and God is substituted for the chasm of dualism, and we never catch the Luciferian sleight of hand. I think Buber's onto something.

There are some puzzles that are only solved because they are unsolvable. Some situations, especially riddles, are perfectly ambiguous and the perfection of that ambiguity becomes a factor in solving the riddle. The perfection of ambiguity betrays intention in the design.

Most of the riddles I know that follow this pattern are so intricate that it would belabor the reader to put them here. But I knew a guy who once prayed, "I don't know what to do. God, you will tell me. I will toss this coin. If it is heads, I will do this. If it is tails, I will do that. Whatever the case, you are responsible for the outcome, and I will know that God is real." As I recall, thirty years later, the matter involved a girl, and no this is not really about me under the hypothetical "friend." The coin was tossed, it landed on its side, and it rolled into a drain. He was furious because he felt toyed with. I saw it as an overwhelming confirmation of God and God's sovereignty. For a moment, I am comforted by the words of Heraclitus: "He who cannot seek the unforeseen is lost, for the known way is an impasse." Of course the riddle is unsolvable. This is hoping in things unseen, and precisely what Tertullian meant, "I believe because it is absurd."

Dualism cannot be understood. It is a question, by design, that cannot be answered. I have tried. I cannot tell you how many days or years of my life. It is wrapped too well into the particulars of my own existence for me to transcend it. More than a mote in my eye, it is the eye itself (and the eye is directly a brain bud). Perhaps the third eye could see it, but that has yet to open. Any attempt to solve the question will pull you in to the system of broken thought that dualism is, like a black hole. The fruit of this tree is poisoned. It is not to be understood; it is to be overcome, and that is within one's soul and not in the world.

The doctrine of creation carries with it that there is God and that which God created. This creates a little hiding place, a place where perversion may enter. The chasm is the perversion of the natural distinction between the Creator and creation; dualism is the perversion of dialectic.

44

If the great evil in the world is dualism, why not answer it with a rigid non-dualism? How come that's not just the answer? There are many questions that follow the assertion of the evil of dualism, and this one is the most obvious. How come we don't just get up there and destroy everything binary? Just smash it like the iconoclasts?

This is worth a little exposition. This is how the lie is spread. This is the "Temptation of Inversion." Dualism is a heavy problem and the self wants to react to that. The soul can feel the oppressive weight of the dualism and a desire for transcendence begins to form. Very quickly that desire for transcendence can be sublimated with an inversion to the opposite polarity. When a right-winger converts to a left-winger, it will seem transcendent, but it isn't.

There are three subtleties here. Just because something is wrong doesn't mean the opposite is right. Just because the Nazis are fighting the Russians doesn't mean that either one of those is on my side. Just because Lenin or Stalin wants to say God is dead and that Himmler is looking for a mythology in the occult that will lift up Lucifer, doesn't mean that either is righteous. The binary decision tree is incapable of consecrating anything; it has no holiness of its own. And it doesn't make us righteous if we fight either one (remember, they are already fighting each other). The enemy of my enemy is quite likely my enemy in this rogue's gallery. It is the Temptation of Inversion because we so want to believe that worship is finding the right devil. It's not.

As an embellishment, the Nazis themselves are this kind of polarizing symbol. Just because the American in the movie is fighting the Nazis doesn't make him righteous. We have an unconscious reaction in *Star Wars* when we discover the enemies are called "stormtroopers." We have feelings about stormtroopers and feelings about those who fight them. But it is unconscious no more. This is the fulcrum behind identity politics and cancel culture. If every opinion of the enemy is wrong, then the opposite appears right *even if it escapes my comprehension entirely*. This is also known as "the Jedi Templar Mind Trick." Part of the way the trick works in the deception that you are in on it, when the joke has always been on you. We laugh at the people onscreen who are fooled by the trick, not realizing we are fooled by our laughter.

The second subtlety is that this is how gnosticism thrives. The gnosticism says yes, this is a battle between good and evil, but we are wrong about who is good and who is evil. Let us be like Nietzsche and transcend good and evil. Let us indulge ourselves and do whatever we want and convince ourselves we are righteous. It doesn't matter if the gods are on top of the titans or the titans are on top of the gods; it's a pagan pantheon either way. The problem of dualism creates an appetite for transcendence, but that appetite is easily satisfied with the assertion of another dualism, particularly if it's upside down.

The third subtlety is the function of the "found phenomena." Meaning, we tend to give things more credence when they are found. But this completely disregards the reality of how the found thing came to be. People have to make tough choices all the time. We whittle the options down to two, and through some rationale we convince ourselves that this is the "better option." But when both options are terrible, what has really happened is that you have been cornered into giving your consent. We like to think our choices are authentic and that our pathway through life is free. I can find this movie or that movie, but both movies were placed there for me to find. Of course they were. Movies don't make themselves. You might turn on or tune into your favorite newscaster who uses a turn of phrase, a buzzword. And it seems perfectly natural and effectively descriptive. This newscaster has helped you find the buzzword. Until you change the station, and they are all talking the same way. No longer is this a random "finding." This is choreography.

The bitter truth here is that dualism is fortified and protected by irony. You can't just reject a dualism as a matter of course without creating new one. Let's say I don't like extremists because they kick people out of the church. How do I answer that? Do I kick them out because they kick people out? If I kick them out, I become what I'm trying to kick out. I've perpetuated the problem instead of solving it.

We see this again and again in the Gospels. Jesus says he does not come to destroy the Law, but to fulfill it. In many ways, that is precisely because if he were to destroy the Law what he would be needing to do it is a new

Law. If we create a new Law, then somebody else would have to come in and destroy that. This is a question to which we must return later.

We see it in the logic of the parables. Usually the parables don't rest, or conclude, in a binary answer. The argument here gets a little sophisticated, because the parables are predicated on a binary world. Many of the parables are entangled, or exploded, logic structures like the Liar Riddle. The Prodigal Son uses the same logic as the Liar Riddle. A man has two sons. One tells the dad he'll help but doesn't. The other says he won't help but does. Evaluate. This is the same entanglement paradigm of the Liar Riddle.

But sometimes the parables seem to reinforce the dualistic ideas of rewards and punishments. I would argue that even in those passages, Jesus is trying to subvert the underlying dualism, but in this case by having "bad things" happen to allegedly "good people." The dualism of Eden remains in his crosshairs, and as Paul suggests, Christ is the "New Adam." Said again, as early as Paul, Jesus is already seen as corrective response to Adam's transgression of eating of the Tree of Dualism.

I can't state this strongly enough. So much of the entirety of the person of Jesus—that is, the birth, death, resurrection, teachings, miracles, and biography of Jesus—is so focused on addressing the problem of dualism, that this is an essential dimension of understanding spiritual midwifery. Midwifery is a mode of helping people toward transcendence, and dualism is a mode of preventing people from it. The world is binary; the path is not. To suggest that the path is binary is the beginning of the idolatry of dualism.

Theologically, I would term religious nondualism as "radical monotheism." It is an expression of submission to God where not even texts, traditions, or theologies about God are held more sacred than God. Some people love the idea of dethroning texts and tradition, but it also means that we can't worship our polarized politics (which have found their way to more than one pulpit). It is a spirituality that does not confuse the blessings and the power of God with God. The creation is utterly distinct from the Creator. And any other conjugation, in fact, would deny that God has the power to create. And people always confuse the gifts of God with the One who gave them. We worship them while we have them, and we curse God when we have to let them go. Every blessing is only on loan.

We find the prohibition against idolatry in Exodus and we also find prohibitions against graven images. I like a subsequent discussion in Exodus 34. "For thou shalt worship no other god: for the LORD, whose name is Jealous, is a jealous God." This is not to say that God is petty. But it is to envelop the command in a metaphor of intimacy and fidelity.

You also see it in the Shema: "Hear, O Israel: the Lord our God, the Lord is one." Jesus actually cites this prayer in Mark when he is asked which commandment is the greatest. "Hear, O Israel; The Lord our God is one Lord: and thou shalt love the Lord thy God with all thy heart, and with all thy soul, and with all thy mind, and with all thy strength." This is the first commandment. One can worship "good." One can worship "evil." One can worship "duality" itself. (And this is typically what one does by worshipping "good," although there are even more abstract ways of worshipping "duality.") One can even worship "nonduality" and make it an idol. Indeed, the nondualistic idols are the most grotesque of all. Jesus is offering something different. This is radical monotheism.

CHAPTER 11

The Fairy Tale

*And we know
that all things work together for good
to them that love God . . .*

PAUL

45

What is the function of a bedtime story? It is to put the children to sleep.

I do not believe in fiction. Or rather, there is, and there is no, such a thing called "fiction." The reader may immediately understand what I mean when I say there is fiction. There is a section of it in the bookstore. Most of our entertainment is packaged fiction. And it generates billions of dollars. All that's real. Right?

I don't think so. There are two kinds of fictional stories; either stories that are handed to us, or stories that we make up. Let's start with the first category. Regarding the stories that are handed to us, things are "presented" rather than "found," although many times they are "presented as found" or, even more mind-boggling, it's found by someone but what they have was "presented as found" (which, if you managed to follow, doesn't mean it was actually found). If you could prove something was truly found that would be more trustworthy because it removes the motives of the presenter. The fictional stories that become our pop culture are either advertising or propaganda. That is what they are.

We tend to trust things that are "presented as found," because the fact that it is found bestows it with credibility. This has a lot to do with how the Church of Reason maintains its role in promulgating the anti-tradition. Children are raised into the tradition to various degrees by their parents. The parents entrust the academy with their children, and the children then trust the academy on the borrowed trust of their parents. The children, by the way, are also becoming adults and they want to individuate from their parents. Then, the academy becomes new *mater*; that is, they are fully matriculated. The academy indoctrinates the anti-tradition and the anti-tradition is trusted as found. Indeed, the student thinks that they themself have found it. As if it were an artifact from their college journey. But all of their fossils were planted and there is nothing new under the sun. It is a fascinating mechanism; its torque comes from the individual confusing choice-making with self-expression and self-actualization. Each person finds their path through a series of steps and choices, and because the path is strung together by a continuous string of experiential days, they are inclined to think that it's real. But, if one were to insert a false choice, a fake choice, then the result is deception.

The "presented as found" phenomenon is how things are sanitized by the marketplace. If the choice itself happens at the market, we are inclined to gloss over how it got to market—the unholy process by which the sausage is made. With such sanitation in effect we too may even aspire to contribute to the marketplace with a product of our own. Especially if our friends have also brought products to market. It would never occur to us that in such a secular sanctuary things have been placed there to do me evil. We can relate to greed. We can't fathom all seven sins and the desire to control.

A word about the propaganda. Imagine a criminal who abducted a person for two hours, put them in a darkened room, forced them into a bizarre, voyeuristic sexual encounter, had them watch seven gruesome murders, and another sexual encounter for good measure, all while shouting their political beliefs—such a criminal would be guilty of espionage-grade torture and attempted brainwashing. Or, the criminal could charge them twenty bucks, give them popcorn and a drink, and call it a day at the movies. Sometimes it's just the sex, sometimes the violence. We also like to mix and match it up. In this culture, we buy our propaganda. We like to pay top dollar for the MK Ultra experience.

Then there are stories that we make up. Kids playing cops and robbers on the playground or a made-up story before bed. Or, I can certainly sit down and write a novel. I would argue that the behavior in children's play or the novel that I write are so integral to the author's psychology that these things are actually autobiography. In this sense, we are not like the Creator. We do not author life. We tell stories that are unrecognizable derivatives of ourselves, but at the end of the day, they are derivatives. So all alleged fiction is either advertising and propaganda, or autobiography and confession.

Let's look at someone like J. K. Rowling, who is interesting because she has now become controversial and means different things to different groups. Before that, she wrote Harry Potter for her son. I would say that was imaginative autobiography. And then, her story became a big movie industry and very commercial. What the franchise now is: something between autobiography and corporate advertising.

This is why I prefer literature before mass media. Then it's only an expression of the psychology of the author. Things like Shakespeare are more complicated because at one point, the Globe Theater was Hollywood, and you can wonder to what degree those plays were also advertising, and maybe even propaganda as well. Shakespeare sold tickets too. And this complexity underlies a lot of the conspiracy of who actually wrote Shakespeare. And why.

Fiction, and what passes for it, is either lies or confession.

Nonfiction is the perfect word for what it describes. One asks, "Is that the truth?" The retort: well, it's certainly nonfiction.

We create worlds. Which is not so much to say that we build the worlds, but that we imagine them. And we often imagine them without knowing we have done so.

This is a power that people have. It is important to address this power here and now, because there is no fairy tale without it. Have you ever been so focused on something that it's the only thing that matters? That is creating a world. Have you ever been so immersed in a chess game that time stopped, and the loss of your queen truly felt catastrophic? It is because you have created a world out of the chess game.

These worlds have coherence and integrity. When your kid strikes the batter out or makes a great out at first, the cheering from the crowd is real. In that moment, your kid really is a hero because in that moment that's what a hero really is.

Growing up in the eighties, we spent hours on the phone, tethered by a telephone wire. All it takes is two voices in a conversation. This, I think, is what Buber means when he says, "All real life is encounter." An encounter is world-creating, even disembodied, even just a voice. Even just a text-based chat. When we share such a created world with another, it is called intimacy.

Sometimes it's so intense that it's the intensity itself that pulls in our focus and thus creates the world. A hot shower can do this. For that matter, cold water does the same thing. A really bad flu can do this. A wound can do this. A trauma can do this. Sex, of course, does this.

Worlds are created for us. This is a little bit of a misnomer. The worlds are not actually created, because the world only exists when we focus on it and bring it to life. But they are staged for us, ready for our imagination to fire up the magic. Theme parks do this well for children, with ambient music and sounds and fake boulders.

There is something slightly sinister about this observation about amusement parks. "Amusement" means if you strip someone of their spiritual muse, they will stay in their containment, dumb and happy. Hence, the parallel for the etymology of "entertainment." Entertainment is a container—a prison. And yes, worlds are created for us, just to keep us busy. Welcome, customer, here's your world.

Remember, fiction is either a lie or confession.

46

We will go from one created world to another. We will go from our home (one world we have created) to work (a world created by another) and that is called a commute. We will go from high school to college, and that is called graduation. We do this all the time, from one societal institution to the next. This is how people are moved along from birth to death, matriculated through life from beginning to end.

We do so with varying degrees of self-awareness and agency. We work to keep pace with our classmates, and when they graduate we do too. Maybe we've really worked at it, or maybe we've just drifted along, but we can't deny that we were complicit in the achievement. We were involved. We left fingerprints.

Occasionally we are moved between worlds without our consent or any involvement whatsoever and that is very jarring. I would even say traumatic. This is Reality Trauma. We often forget that we can be objectified that way and moved around at somebody's whim. Maybe we didn't even know it was possible. This leads to massive disorientation and derealization. We always think we are living at the base level of reality, not seeing our role in world creation. Immediately this produces painful questions for us. Like Neo, "I have all these memories of my life that are not real. What does that mean?" While Neo himself knows that the noodles are not real, I think he says this because we are fooled into thinking they are real because they are found—and found by us. Finding things gives them credence, because we think that the discovery is an inoculation against deception.

This is a little more horrific in *The Truman Show*. If your entire life context is staged, how are you real inside that environment? Are you? This is a very serious question. We are tempted to discount *The Truman Show* as a fairy tale, but so much of what we trust has been staged.

The term "Reality Trauma" is not a throwaway term. The trauma is real, as are the symptoms. The only treatment I have found is Radical Monotheism.

So, we are duped. But just because the things do not mean all that we think they do does not make them meaningless. But it is genuinely disorienting. It really did mean something when my kid made the out at first base. Even if it's all fake, even if baseball itself is fake (which it is) my kid made a great catch. But it was a relative meaning, not an absolute one. Only God is absolute.

It is strange and horrifying to lose faith in fiction. Much of what passes for my culture is product, either propaganda or advertising. I was driving down the road when it really hit me. What does it mean when nothing is real? It was during the pandemic. I was listening to "Smoke on the Water." You know you're old when what was "heavy metal" is for the fortysomethings at the grocery store. You should not be able to buy yogurt to Quiet Riot. I noticed it decades ago, when rock was no longer rebellion but now niche. For the record, niche is where you keep the dead. But I know it happened before I noticed it. Where commercialization and corporate contracts killed the garage band. And now classic rock radio stations play nostalgic pop music just to break up the rhythm. It may be rock and roll to Billy Joel, but he was never rock to me.

What does it mean when everything that you thought was cool was really product? Is anything cool? Is anything real?

But, man, that's a really good riff. Relatively speaking, of course.

47

Sometimes I talk about living in two worlds, and going between worlds. This is an acquired taste. I go entirely between distinct worlds, completely from one to the next, and I am wont to spend considerable time in the space between.

One thing that I have noticed from that position is the degree to which people live in overlapping concentric worlds. It is their ability to do this that allows them to move around and be matriculated into different worlds without noticing a transition. If third and fourth grade are presented as both being in the world of elementary school, going from one to the next seems little more than a natural step up. The experience of sustaining concentric worlds is expressed in the idiom "walking and chewing gum at the same time." These are fairly distinct human capacities, and it may take some practice to get the hang of it. I described it on the child level by going through elementary school. On the adult level, it's like stepping out of a business meeting to mediate a conflict between the kids. On the one hand, doing a good job as a parent means keeping the job and keeping the peace at home. On the other hand, doing a good job as an employee means doing something to keep your phone from exploding and being able to bring your full attention to the meeting. This is the dynamic and tension of concentric worlds. This is the film *Life is Beautiful*—perhaps the best prison film of all.

This is how the battle is fought. It is a war of context. It is a war of one set of parentheses within the next.

Things will go bad (unless we can see that there is another good (which may also contain things we don't like). We only discover the full meaning when we escape the Final Parenthesis. Indeed, people think that the final punctuation of life is a period, or that the apocalypse itself is an explosive exclamation point, but I say to you that the great meaning at the end of time is the Great Parenthesis. This is what it means when it says: "And we know that all things work together for good to them that love God . . ." This does not mean that really awful things do not happen to those who love God. They certainly do, take it from a hospital chaplain. But God holds the greatest context. Indeed, even the worst day brings us one day closer to the fulfillment of God's plan. The question is, how are you going to work it? How good is your chess? The bad things are redeemed one parenthesis at a time. Is this the story of Good Friday, Easter Sunday, or the second coming?)

Rest assured, the second coming is the Final Parenthesis.

About chess. If you can master the dynamic of the concentric worlds, it can appear as if you are doing magic. Chess is a turn-based game. White gets to move and black responds. Only then can white move again. But if black can move in such a way as to threaten two pieces at once, even though one possibility excludes the other, it is very much the same as if you moved two pieces instead of one. It is unstoppable because you are playing the game at a higher level. This is two ways to win at tic-tac-toe. Both cannot be blocked. One person is defeated by the impossibility and irony of doing two things at once, and another person is victorious because they have transcended it. Paul uses this kind of logic all the time. If people are preaching Christ with bad intent or preaching with good intent, it really doesn't matter because Christ is being preached either way. The transcendent always wins. If Paul is being supported in prison or in spirit, he is being supported either way. If to live is Christ and to die is gain, life becomes a no-lose scenario.

To then develop this a little further, there is a problematic tension here between the possibility of living in concentric worlds (stacked worlds) and the human capability to create worlds. The tension is that if the worlds become too stacked and there is just too much happening at once, the human capacity to create worlds is just stymied and flooded and the individual feels like they are lost in the cosmos. I think of Dick Van Dyke from *Mary Poppins* wearing the one-man band costume. A musician finds a world within a single instrument. Van Dyke manages to effect something resembling a tune without collapsing into complete noise. This amazes me for far more than a second. He's a singer and dancer pretending to be a British jack-of-all-trades who is poor. He's pretending to come from the underside of London. He's doing a movie. And he has his own life, his own religion, his own story. He's flapping his arms and moving his legs. All of these worlds are performed at once, and yes, it does seem like magic.

What is real about this performance? Is it not a fiction within a fiction within a fiction? Is that what "authentic" means?

48

What is a fiction?

Here: Once upon a time, there was a funny, old man who sometimes walked with a cane. Sometimes he didn't walk at all. He was with a wife and two daughters. And a dog. One day, he was taking the dog for a walk, and thought, tomorrow I will go out on a short journey, and get some things that we need.

So he rose the next morning, and went out, pretty much as planned, pretty much like you would expect. When he returned he could not find anyone.

He began to search. He went into his youngest daughter's room. She loved her dolls, they were her favorite thing. Everything was in place, just like she liked to keep it. But the man looked closely. There was an extra doll. And stranger still, this doll bore a remarkable resemblance to his daughter. "Sweetie, is that you?" He heard a wolf howl in the distance.

It was her. In his heart of hearts he knew it to be true. Somehow, amongst the raggedy dolls, his daughter had turned into a doll. She had been sitting at a pretend tea, and with that awareness the doll tipped over as sometimes dolls do. The old man picked her up and kissed her. He took out his chess set, and arranged it before her. He told her the names of the pieces. And they would play. Of course, he had to reach across and take the doll's hand to move the pieces. After some time, she came back to being a girl. Like the nutcracker, she had become the general of a mighty army.

The wolf howled again. The man requested to take leave of the general. Permission granted. He looked for his eldest daughter, his firstborn. She too was gone. But the door was open. Feeling the draft, the old man stepped outside and shut the door only to see something furry out of the corner of his eye. He took a look and spied the wolf. He followed the wolf for about a half mile. She had made a den. It was getting dark and cold, so he tried to go into the den. She snarled. He noticed the necklace. It was his other daughter. He made a smooth spot on the ground, trying to put together a nest or a shelter. It was cold, but he slept there. In the middle of the night, he found a warm wolf sleeping against him. In the morning, he fed the wolf and found his daughter again.

Still, there was one left. He went into the bedroom. He could not find anything but hay, straw, and hoof prints. It had been a strange day. His one daughter had been a doll, his other a wolf. Why shouldn't his wife be a horse? The only herd was a few miles up the road. When he found the herd, he was dismayed. He was not a horseman and they all looked the same. He tried to inspect each horse, but he could not even distinguish between those he had inspected and those he had not. Surrounded by horses, he didn't know what to do. Then, one approached him and bit him on the arm. That was her! He led her home, and by the time they arrived they were hand in hand.

The next day he was very reluctant to go back out. But after horse wrangling and sleeping with wolves and facing the general, they needed more things. So he went back out. But this day went very badly. He found himself completely lost.

The general, though, knew what to do. She rallied the troops. She got her sister to lead a search and rescue party, and her time among the wolves had made her a capable tracker that could catch anything. She found and caught the old man and brought him home. His wife made sure that he, and the entire herd, were fed.

CHAPTER 12

The Name

> The Tao that can be told is not the eternal Tao.
> The name that can be named is not the eternal name.
> The nameless is the beginning of heaven and Earth.
> The named is the mother of the ten thousand things.
> Ever desireless, one can see the mystery.
> Ever desiring, one sees the manifestations.
> These two spring from the same source but differ in name;
> this appears as darkness.
> Darkness within darkness.
> The gate to all mystery.
>
> Lao Tzu
>
> 49

Names are very, very interesting, and especially forbidden names. My mind always jumps to Moses and forbidden names. I believe that some names are forbidden because they are powerful, and other names are forbidden because they are impossibly ineffable, and sometimes both.

It is more than quaint that Adam's first job was to name the things of creation. I like to say his first job was that of a poet, and that this is fitting work to follow a God who creates by speaking. Adam must toil by putting words to things.

Like Lao Tzu, Heraclitus comes fast to mind: "The One, the only wisdom, does and does not consent to be called Zeus." Every time I think of these words, I see a different angle. And we will come back to these words again, but this time the awareness rings so clear: There is One who consents, and there is Zeus, and they are not the same. And we can pronounce Zeus, but if there is a name for the unknown One, it is not ours to pronounce.

Names are powerful, and this is one of the hardest chapters to confess.

A person receives many names during the course of a lifetime. These are given names and they must be given. That is, they only have meaning or power when they are given to us, and such power is derived from the giver. Most of these names say something about the relationship. I call these vow-related names because somewhere along the line, a vow was nearby. I worked really hard to get the name "husband," but it was only my wife who gave it to me, and there was a vow just around the corner. A vow, mind you, before God, and therefore my commitment is to God and to my wife.

There are other vows that stem from this vow, like promises. I promised my daughter that I would be her dad when she was born. This is the name father. She was an outright promise, and very connected to the vow to my wife. My own parents made me a son and they gave me that name, and of course I can't remember what was said, but if I understand how these things work there was a vocation and vow in there too. I have held most of the engendered names possible for me. I have also held the name of friend, and this is a name that is much more easily given without the formality of vows.

I have struggled with the given names, all of them. I have had some complicated feelings around those. I will say that these names have been challenging for me, but that seems par. My mother once said in astonishment, "Nothing is easy for you." She has this way of being suddenly honest. I like to think I get some of my straight shooting from her. I was a teenager and furious when she said it and I was furious because she was right. I did not want her to be right. Anyone would try something if they knew they couldn't fail. I like to ask the question, "What is so important to you that you would do it if you knew you were going to fail, and die trying?" Most people are hard-pressed to answer this question, and if they can the answer is usually one of the vow-related given names. That's how I answer. Thus, my struggle with the given names is how I have died trying.

My challenge is that in describing my difficulty with given names, I have to take exquisite care not to give myself a new name. At some point, I have loved everyone who has given me a given name, including the bullies because the bullies would not have had so much power had I not loved them. And I wish that I could have made everyone I have loved aware of the love that they created in me. I have loved those names, especially the family names.

With some measure of catharsis, I will say that I really think that much of my complicated feeling stems from an experience of frustrated gratitude. I have been given far more blessings than I deserve in this life, especially from those who have given me the given names. I have tried to live my life as a way of saying, "Thank you." Usually, in the transaction of human kindness acknowledgment balances the debt. In my case, I am left short with a sense of poverty.

At one point, my name was simply "good." I have no recollection of that and that's extremely hard to remember. Most of my life, I would gladly have received "good enough," which I may always work at. My name could have been anything. I could have been Christopher, or Larry, even Rob, or anything. As it turns out, I was given Stephen.

I am named for Stephen the Martyr, a truthteller, and maybe a few of those who kept his name alive through kindness. According to tradition, he is also the first deacon. This is also my station and it pleases me to at least share this. The apostle Paul was present at Stephen's stoning while he was named Saul. Stephen was stoned for telling the truth, and not very nicely. "You guys could use a good circumcision." That's never a crowd-pleaser.

The Faller is kind of interesting. Most people have some kind of genetic link to their family name. If your last name is Shoemaker, you're probably the son of a Shoemaker, or Baker, or something.

I have no genetic tie to my name; this is another gift of being adopted. It is with a certain irony that I am named Faller. I have significant trouble walking, and I fall a lot. My knees and elbows exist only as scar tissue. So, of all things, "Faller." I appreciate the joke. It's something to laugh at and it feels a little affectionate. Maybe kissed by the ground instead of crushing or crashing. I have often said that this is God's little joke, and that my own *halacha* has had more to do with violence against the ground than I have enjoyed. Walking across any room is much more a tightrope experience than I would like; plastic Legos are like firewalking. My Olympian hubris is daring to cross the room first thing out of bed, and I feel like an Olympic gymnast every time I can stick the landing without falling. For my part, I'm glad that God and I have a joking relationship because I only joke with my best friends. My students know I love them when I tease them. And there have been many, many things about my life that have been extremely frustrating, but it has been hilarious. Thanks be to God. Sometimes people in my immediate vicinity wonder why I laugh so much. But it is either laugh or cry; Democritus or Heraclitus, and only here do I prefer Democritus. Only here.

(A small side note, my love of humor, bad humor, irony, puns, and the dreaded dad joke, I think, originates from my predisposition to nondualism. Nondualism is necessary for every double *entendre*. You have to be able to hear things in more than one way at once. This has made me a better chaplain because I'm not locked in to what I think the patient must be saying. I am open to the strangeness of their truth, and I have to constantly clarify and rarify my understanding of what they tell me. Sometimes, if it's really funny you can hear one thing in many ways. The best jokes ricochet. When does a joke become a dad joke? When the punch line becomes apparent.)

I look for loftier etymologies. The name could have been "one who returns in the fall" (there is something of an implied circuit rider in that, or at least something seasonal). It could also be "one who fells trees." Possibly the menacing "one who fells his adversary." There are humorous Western overtones of confusing "feller" and "fellow." My mind makes jokes like this constantly. People may find it hard to be around me, but I find hilarity in everything.

At any rate there are, actually, a few "Stephen Fallers" out there. It's kind of eerie when you can Google your own tombstone. There is also a jewelry retailer in Galway that shares my name, but I do not think my family has any Irish roots.

My father's father was not raised by his father. That is my lineage. My grandfather was raised by his uncle, Uncle Bo. My grandfather was a wandering soul, who would hop a freight train when necessary. He died before I was born.

I have three friends who are absolutely unrelated to ministry or chaplaincy. Total. I had more. Some have died. Much of this is due to my marginal life, and this has completely metastasized at this point. Besides, they are scattered across the continent. Fortunately, we can talk on the phone, but it is as likely as not that I will ever see them again. That alone is interesting and telling that I should find my friends only outside of any real space.

What I want to stress is that the world is full of people and very few call me "Steve." It is also true that philosophy and spirituality have been very significant dimensions of those lifelong friendships. None of them were surprised I went into chaplaincy.

I am extremely appreciative of every kindness that was ever expressed in my direction. While my current number of living friends has achieved an oddly trinitarian status, many people have befriended me over the years. This is something that I have always deeply cherished. Whenever God put people in my path I loved them deeply. I can only hope that this is something I will be able to express in the next life, because I was not able to in this one.

I do have colleagues, and a lot of those, and many of whom I love. If I love them, aren't they friends? Well, we only connect around the ministry or the chaplaincy. Clergy relationships are strange that way. People who want to establish that I'm not their chaplain call me "Stephen." Most everybody else calls me Chaplain or Faller, if I am called anything. Many of the people I encountered have no name for me at all and no need for one.

50

The name that I chose is Chaplain. Not everyone chooses a name. Chaplain is my name; it is how I identify. More than who I am, it is who I choose to be. Who I have chosen to be. As my daughter says, it's what you call me when I'm not in the room. It communicates how I relate to God and how I relate to you.

I don't know a lot of clergy who carry it this way. I am not a clergy who says, "No, no, no, please call me by my first name." Maybe when you have one hand that works this is how you carry things and spread the load. I don't load it that way and have no desire to. A lot of clergy try to have a life outside their ministry and talk about things like "work-life balance"—for good reason. I know chaplains who deride the social worker by calling her "social worker" every time they don't want to be called "chaplain." Not me. I can't see what that gets you. My name is Chaplain; that is my vow. I can only say that if I was going to have any kind of a journey with commitments it was going to look like this.

I am very, very curious to see how deep this goes. "Traveling every path, you would not exhaust the limits of the soul, so deep is its Logos." That's Heraclitus. What words can be substituted for Logos? Nature. Logic. Logo. Name. Path. Wisdom.

When I get to the end, I want to know how far I could have gone. Which path do I want: every. There's only one way to do that. If you want to see how far you can go before you utterly collapse, you are going to have to allow yourself to utterly collapse. There's no other way. Said a little more provocatively, without that collapse, most people live in fear of their limits. You hit your limits by letting them hit you in the face. And then you turn the other cheek. That is the wisdom gift of being a frequent faller.

As a chaplain, I know that nothing is forever. The day will come when I lay down my chaplaincy and that will be fine too. I will give up writing and go back to the knotting of rope. I didn't meet my parents until I was a month old, so I was born without a name, and there will be one waiting for me when I get where I'm going.

CHAPTER 13

The Harrowing

I believe in God the Father Almighty,
Maker of heaven and earth:
And in Jesus Christ his only Son our Lord,
Who was conceived by the Holy Ghost,
Born of the Virgin Mary,
Suffered under Pontius Pilate,
Was crucified, dead, and buried:
He descended into hell;
The third day he rose again from the dead;
He ascended into heaven,
And sitteth on the right hand of God the Father Almighty;
From thence he shall come to judge the quick and the dead.
I believe in the Holy Ghost;
The holy Catholic Church;
The Communion of Saints;
The Forgiveness of sins;
The Resurrection of the body,
And the Life everlasting.
Amen.

51

I love this part of the tradition. It's not even in the Bible. It's the Apostles' Creed. Every time I hear it and say it, I am always delighted that the defining acts of Christ are passive. Born, suffered, crucified, dead, buried—even ascended—these things happened to Christ, even upon Christ. The motif resonates with another part of the liturgy called the Mystery of Faith: Christ has died, Christ has resurrected, Christ will come again. For all of our striving and doing, the holiest of events happen without lifting a finger.

There's the part about the church which is incorporated under the section on the Holy Spirit. This component probably has a lot to do with why the creed survived this long.

My absolutely favorite part is "He descended into Hell." This is its own source of conjecture and debate. Some people read this to mean that Jesus was dead in the ground for three days, but there's a lot of tradition that says Jesus actually went to hell and freed people like the righteous pagans that would have otherwise been Christian if they had the opportunity in life. It may be the church's first step toward documented interfaith ministry.

So, the harrowing is not in the Bible, but there are glimpses of this. While this is not meant to be an exhaustive study, I do like these verses. From 1 Peter 3:18, "For Christ also hath once suffered for sins, the just for the unjust, that he might bring us to God, being put to death in the flesh, but quickened by the Spirit: By which also he went and preached unto the spirits in prison; Which sometime were disobedient, when once the longsuffering of God waited in the days of Noah, while the ark was a preparing, wherein few, that is, eight souls were saved by water."

Yeah. That's one sentence.

And then Paul in Ephesians 4:8: "When he ascended up on high, he led captivity captive, and gave gifts unto men. (Now that he ascended, what is it but that he also descended first into the lower parts of the earth? He that descended is the same also that ascended up far above all heavens, that he might fill all things.)"

Paul has another remark about netherworld Jesus. From Philippians: "That at the name of Jesus every knee should bow, of things in heaven, and things in earth, and things under the earth; And that every tongue should confess that Jesus Christ is Lord, to the glory of God the Father."

If Moses is the archetype of the chaplain's journey, the harrowing of hell is the Christotype. Forget about the Light-Bearer, the Lucifer. Give me the Christ-bearer, the Christopher. Moses takes the people from a captive land to the promised land. Jesus breaks into jail in order to break the captives out. In Luke, Jesus exhorts the disciples to proclaim deliverance to the captives. How do you do that if you don't go where they are? Willie Sutton comes to mind. Why do you rob banks? "Because that's where the money is." Why go to hell? Because that's where the people are.

There is something utterly compelling about these characters between the worlds, whether it's Meatloaf or *Constantine* or *Ghost Rider*, regardless of the melodramatic and ridiculous ways they are presented.

My ministry happens at no temple, no Gothic cathedral. Today, our vaulted structures are shrines to our fear of sickness, suffering, and death. These are our monuments. And that is where I go; the caves where people crawl to die. I go there daily. I tell the students that they are in the belly of the whale; indeed, they are swallowed.

For most of my ministry I have worked on locked units. My first experience was in 1996, and really it has been a mainstay, the better part of twenty-six years at this point. A psychiatric hospital was a part of the Center for Pastoral Care, and I was there nine years.

There is this stupid joke of which I will regale you. What's the difference between psych patients and the staff? The staff have keys.

I do not like the joke because there is a spiritual smarmy quality. "Oh, ho, ho, we are so nutty, and zany, and we have keys, and the patients don't." It is postured as self-effacing, but I am turned off by the pretense of self-awareness and the fact that the joke rests in privilege.

Has it occurred to you, oh funny mental health tech, oh witty unit secretary, oh clever administrator that I never see after orientation, that the patient has something you do not? Namely: a discharge plan. As for you and your superior self, I'll see you on Monday. Every Monday. Forever. Until the end of time. They are going on with their lives: healing and rebuilding. Are you? I hope the pay is worth it. I hope your overlord of a middle manager doesn't take advantage of you. Go ahead and swipe right behind your desk, and pray that someone would love you.

More than once, I have asked myself, "What does it mean that God has put me on locked units for twenty-five years?" Or if not on them, between them. Patients discharge. Students graduate. Am I so utterly remedial as to stay here forever?

52

Sartre says hell is other people. He's not wrong. In whatever zoo this is, we do not treat each other well. We take the human condition and make it worse.

An important concept in this is the pyramid, and of which we are not sufficiently suspicious. We buy into it all the time. But we know better.

If a friend asks us, "Should I invest in this marketing business?" We say, "Absolutely not! It is a 'pyramid scheme!'" But our common sense stops there. We have rescued our friend from a big mistake, then we return to our apartment without recognizing that the entire complex bears an uncanny resemblance to Giza.

Do you see the light? The light at the end of the tunnel? Do you hear the train coming?

Why would we accept belonging to a terrible system? We are middle-managers all, except for two, the guy at the top and the guy at the very bottom. I don't know who the guy at the bottom is, because he is constantly being crushed, killed, and replaced by someone else. We accept our role as middle manager because we find ourselves somewhere in the middle. Coyly, the top looks closer than it is because of the foreshortened perspective: almost within reach, but there is still room. Like a great timeshare in hell, we might be able to get into it if we act now.

That's looking up. Don't look up. Looking down, it could always be worse. Rest assured, there is always some sad sack a little sadder than you. It is a peculiar condescension and obligatory gratitude, and mandatory gratitude never feels very grateful. There is always some tortured class worse off than you. There is always some marginalized group more marginal than you. If you're an immigrant from a bad country, there could be a worse country. If you're uneducated, at least you're not sick. If you're sick, at least you've got your hands. If you don't have your hands, at least you have your feet. The striations are endless.

Your role, as whatever middle manager you are, is to protect your spot. You want to go toward the top of the pyramid, not the bottom. Like hell itself, there's always more room at the base of the pyramid. That's not the direction anyone wants to go, and some of the upper tiers can be pretty comfortable. You get to break some of the rules, and you get the upper-shelf version of healthcare and justice and things. To someone from the bottom, it seems like heaven. You protect your spot by "doing unto others before they do unto you." This is the Pyrite Rule. It looks golden, but it's not. But that is how you get the promotion.

A word about the Pyrite Rule. With its acknowledgement of dualism, never has Orwell's *1984* seemed so prophetic. The hero, Winston, is tortured. He gives up his beloved and says, "Do it to Julia! Do it to her!" And those are the magic words. Satisfied, the overlords withdraw.

There was a real person. Some say the real Indiana Jones. Of course, you can read and read about the fanlore of Indiana Jones and never find him. His name is Otto Rahn. He had a name. He was retained by the Nazis to find the Holy Grail. He traced the grail legend to the Cathars (which was a medieval Christian gnostic movement). We don't know really what Otto Rahn found, or why he believed he would, but I don't think we would. Lots of other names come up as plausible inspirations for the character, but given his fictional context with the Nazis, Rahn is a unique likelihood for the character basis. Rahn even had the look; he wore fedora hats. When he failed to please his masters, he was reassigned as guard duty at the Dachau concentration camp in 1937. It's worth noting that he was gay. And one wonders how Indiana coped with the imprisonment of other gays. But you have to hold on to what you have, right? It can always be worse, right? It doesn't marry very well with John Williams's soaring "Raiders March." I don't know the truth about secret societies, the Knights Templar, and the Cathar movement, but I know Otto Rahn was a real man, and in a real way, he was a prisoner at Dachau. I am amazed at the details of his life, that this fictionalized person cared about dualism like I do, that he became a gnostic and wrote about it.

(This is another bedtime story. Indiana Jones is a very interesting footnote on the harrowing of hell. The harrowing of the underworld is very much the climactic conclusion of *Temple of Doom*. There are reasons for these fictions. In a later film, Indiana Jones revisited his past in a time-traveling adventure. There is a reason for that fiction too.)

What happens if you oppose the pyramid? You get crushed. But even if you were to succeed in your opposition, nothing would happen. Like a child's hourglass, the whole system would invert and we would be entertained by watching the sand flow through from one spot to the other. Within seconds, we would forget that the pyramid had inverted at all. From time to time, the pyramid is inverted and it can take centuries for the sand to reset. But the toy, and the grip, have not changed.

53

I got into a difficult conversation with one of my friends. What does it mean to use the word "prison"? Meaning, some things are gained, some lost, and the terminology is meaningful.

My friend accused me, "If everything is a prison, isn't that just reality then?" I think it's an interesting objection. If absolutely everything we know is a prison, and the term applies equally to everything, does it really mean anything? If the most comfortable and the least comfortable are in a prison, does the term mean anything at all?

I think it does.

If we are talking about a prison, what do we do with this information? How do we relate to it?

My friend asked me, "Is there such a thing as a prison that you can't see?"

I think there is. Some people know they are behind bars. They are denied the illusion that they are not. This is how low they are in the pyramid; if you are low enough you know you are there. But there are lots of bars and locked doors. There are bars at the state prison in Trenton. There are also bars at the gated communities in Princeton. And where I live, we don't use bars to keep people out. We use property taxes. The dog is behind a fence. It may be an invisible fence, but an invisible fence is still a fence. Step out of line and you are going to know that shock collar.

I want to explore our response to the prison, but I want to first go a little deeper into the seen and unseen. There are many social structures, like property taxes, which are not immediately evident in how they segregate communities. I live in a very progressive region. The signs in the yards signal that with undeniable clarity. But we rely on unseen fences.

Some of these are veiled by complexity and bureaucracy, and we're not going to understand them unless we come from the right question or the wrong experience. Why should property values increase every year? By magic? Why shouldn't we suddenly own million-dollar homes? We get more equity, the state gets a bigger tax base, everybody wins, right? No. But these are the things hidden by complexity. Veiled.

Some of the bars are hidden because we don't want to know that they are there. The Eighth Amendment to the United States Constitution prohibits "cruel and unusual punishments" from being inflicted. But we all know that prison sex is real, and that prison justice is real. These are, in fact, active components of the justice system. People are sent to these terrible places where these things happen, knowing that there is nothing to really prevent them, and these outcomes are part of the sentence. Different personae are more or less at liberty to express their satisfaction about prison justice. You won't hear it from the judge, but you will hear it from family members of the victim.

So, yes, there can be an invisible prison. Visibility is overrated. If it's there, what do we do about it?

A lot of this depends on our relative position to the prison. We might like to imagine these relative positions in the context of a military rescue operation, like a bad episode of *The A-Team*. Send in the commandoes, rescue the hostages, and escape. But this is not how it is. This fantasy is significantly out of phase with the underlying reality.

Let's say that we decide that Trenton is a bad place. I have feelings about judgments like that, but let's just go off the assumption. What do we do about that? We get buses? Get everybody on a bus? What if they don't want a bus? And if they did, where do you send them? Newark? How's that going to go? Camden? Princeton? How's that going to go? Are we just moving the whole prison, part and parcel? This isn't a war-torn country. This is not an afflicted community of a mass shooting. You can't just solve this with a yard sign of solidarity. Flying a flag is only that: flying a flag.

The problem is, as much as we want to distance ourselves from suffering, we are not in Jesus' position in the harrowing of hell. We don't have the keys. It takes an insane amount of privilege to think that you do have the keys. We don't have the buses. We don't have anywhere to take them to. It's Egypt everywhere. We are in the world that we need to extricate from. We are a part of it. We want to be the heroic Allies, but we are in the camps.

This is why the prayer says: deliver us from evil. We cannot deliver ourselves from it. We need deliverance and safe passage.

I have heard it said that the problem follows the word. If you use "prison" you make yourself a "prisoner." By your own thought project. People do get in their own way, but this seems particularly cruel to me, a way of eternally blaming the victim. As if the prisoner spoke his prison into existence. An interesting counterargument can be made that one is equally imprisoned by proclaiming oneself free when the reality is otherwise. Agree with me or not, I don't know why the alternative is so hard to swallow: that the perversion and corruption of free will necessarily means stealing or trading the free will of others. If we have the power, we will imprison and enslave each other. That seems pretty obvious.

But our relative position is sure and insecure. We are not visiting the zoo; we are the zoo. The question is only: what does one prisoner say to another? Any kind of liberation operation has to start from there.

So, I say that the word *prison* is a meaningful term. It doesn't add any detail of definition; like I said, it's Egypt everywhere. And the meaning of the term doesn't even describe the Creator. This is the problem of the lie all over again. If creation is fallen, and if creation everywhere is a prison, we really can't know if it's because it's fallen or because it's designed that way (like maybe the Cathars would think).

But the term does give us one thing. As long as we have it, there is the possibility of liberation. The word *prison* gives us the possibility of fulfilling Scripture. "The Spirit of the Lord is upon me, because he hath anointed me to preach the gospel to the poor; he hath sent me to heal the brokenhearted, to preach deliverance to the captives, and recovering of sight to the blind, to set at liberty them that are bruised . . ."

54

I was crushed when I got to college.

I had been told things that I wanted to hear. I was told that when I got to college, people would see me for who I really am. Very specifically, that they would look past my wheelchair, and that I would be able to find friendships and love and romance, and that like the rest of the world, I would be able to participate in the human condition. What Søren calls, "The Universal."

When I got there, I realized that there was no magic switch for people. It took a few months for me to realize it. They don't reach a certain age and then live completely differently. If anything, college was high school part two. Like a bad sequel.

What can be deceptive is that adults may befriend a precocious child. They may open themselves for genuine discourse. And that possibility is very refreshing. You can come away from those adults, as I did, very much with the false belief that this kind of society is possible.

In reality it doesn't work that way. In hindsight, there are a dozen reasons why the adults don't recognize the precocious disabled child now grown up. Children don't count. They can be ignored easily. They are not equals, and they certainly are not sexual equals.

But when you are the adult, sexual and disabled, you become more threatening, not less.

I felt so cheated when I figured it out. I had endured my adolescent depression in the hopes that life could change and that the adult world was different.

I went to the bathroom in my freshman dorm and cried. I would say "ran" but I don't run anywhere and I crashed through the door with my wheelchair, probably at full speed. The catalyst had been a college party, which I experienced as dreadful. It was a spectacle of lechery, and men and women wanted to be there with each other, and you couldn't hear a word. No dialogue allowed.

But, something happened that day that probably set the course of my life. It probably put me on the path toward ministry, even though I was working through my freshman doubts and my faith was under construction. I made a vow. My vow was simple. If they would not let me be one of them, then my vow was to help them, even defiantly. Not because I was better, not because I would educate them or improve them. Probably because I'm deeply oppositional. They pushed me out, and I would push in. If you reject me with stupid hate, I will love you—just for spite and defiance. It was how I chose to attach myself to the human race. I would belong in the "space between spaces," and find out what the creative possibilities were in the margins.

The result of this is that exile is no longer a threat. It is one less means of control. As well with the threat of disrespect and dehumanization. And I am that much more free. This is the space where I was able to stage my counteroffensive and plan the prison break. It may be Egypt everywhere, we may all be prisoners, but at least in solitary there is the luxury of getting the chance to put your thoughts together.

The wardens and the guards with their towers and their yards do not like what happens in the margin. Floodlight may break the night, spotlight might burn with spite, but the margin may they never take. The margin is my own, this old dog his bone, and in it, I but my God am alone. At last free, first I see that which is mine is me. Moon may shine; my soul is mine, meant for Thine, in the margin be. The wardens and the guards with their towers and their yards do not like what happens in the margin.

CHAPTER 14

The Road

A certain man went down from Jerusalem to Jericho,
and fell among thieves,
which stripped him of his raiment,
and wounded him, and departed,
leaving him half dead.

55

In another place, I have quoted Frost. Today, I am aware of the implicit danger of the road.

One of my favorite inspirational stories belongs to Canadian Rick Hansen. He was a paraplegic athlete who raised awareness and money for his cause by taking his wheelchair on a twenty-six-month world tour, attempting to cross every continent. This is also the story behind the song "Man in Motion."

The truth is, I love roads. For a moment, I think of the poem that begins, "Two roads diverged down a yellow wood . . ." I probably fell in love with roads because of Rosaryville Road and especially where it connected with Route 301. This was my first commute. I took it through elementary school, middle school, and high school. I learned to drive on it. I could sleep on it, and sleeping alone, I knew every bend, bump, and curve. I took it twice a day for about ten years. And then, knowing as way leads on to way, I never went back.

Driving is probably the only thing that I do that is effortless, whether it's a car, van, or my wheelchair. For a brief moment, I get to partake in the space and observe it without fighting it. I am so tired of fighting.

My father's father was not raised by his father. He did, however, start a company that would be responsible for building the beltway around DC. It is a peculiar legacy because millions of people travel it every day, but nothing there bears his name. I am touched that this man who could hop a train in the thirties could succeed to build the beltway.

I like roads because with no moving parts they take you places. They themselves are in-between spaces. The roads between nodes. Like the *bardo* or *barzakh* it lies like an isthmus between real places. You spend time on the road, you know the road. You see it at different times of the day with different angles of the sun and in different seasons of the year. It reminds us that we are all but travelers; that we are all passing through.

When my kids were weaning, I'd sleep in the car with them. I couldn't pick them up and jiggle them, and my wife couldn't either because they would never stopped crying if she was near them. I'd slip the car into drive and do just that. We watched the dawn break and dodged the deer. Altogether for both kids, it was six months to a year. Life is a highway. Those were not bad days.

Roads are the most dangerous place I go, and where I spend much time.

56

Over the years, I have had the opportunity to experiment with this, but the context of the experiment requires a little setup. I was at an event called National Clinical Training Seminar, which was just a regional chaplaincy conference. At each NCTS there was a group activity call Tavistock (sometimes it was called group relations). This activity was a product of the "encounter culture" of the seventies. "Tavistock" was a theoretical method that produced a lot of the theory for group psychology. In these exercises, people would sit in a spiral and people could experiment with saying whatever they wanted to say. It was an invigorating exercise, and the closest thing that this motley crew of interfaith chaplains had to a sacrament.

Tavistock was a fixture of NCTS, and I began using it in a focused way in 2008. I wanted to figure out how I could help the group do its work; in short my question was: what is the spiritual midwifery of groups? So, for about ten years I experimented intentionally with the midwifery of groups. Most people don't bring any intention to the exercise, and one of my colleagues would routinely criticize me. "It feels like you are not one of us," he would say. I hadn't realized that was an option.

There were two years where they modified the exercise. In regular Tavistock (and I should be clear that what happened here was not pure theory or tradition, but something that had emerged unique to the community of NCTS) people can say whatever they want. Freedom is encouraged. In these modified exercises, people were free to form their own groups and explore the possibilities of self-selected subgroups. This was called "intergroup." When the intergroup "rules" were established, groups had to be at least three people, and there were "authorized" rooms of the conference center where those groups were allowed to meet. I understood the intergroup to be a kind of hyper-Tavistock event. Where in normal Tavistock, individuals can say whatever they want, in intergroup groups could form and do whatever they wanted. Beyond that, we were required to follow the laws of the land, New Jersey.

One other thing. For about twenty minutes, they went over what it meant to live in a "world turned upside-down." That was the theme of the conference. It now seems silly to write those words in reference to anything before COVID-19. But it was practically a sermon, like one would expect to hear in a church or a lecture heard in an academic lecture hall. My question is, why prime the group that way? If this is supposed to be a transformative learning event about the group dynamics of the chaplaincy organization, why inject its DNA with these values of being displaced and victimized?

Time to roll up the sleeves. I wanted to try to create the smallest group possible. I had tried the intergroup exercise the year before, and my experiment failed, because my group was too big. I would go with three.

I am also a bit of a character; I have a reputation and it's not entirely good. Again this is where the NCTS construct deviates from the theory. In theory these exercises are consecrations to the holy "here and now." That is, the only thing that matters is the present moment. In practice, these gatherings have memory and people remember you from the last time, and you have to manage that. There is an awful lot of "there and then."

Which three? What would be the purpose of the subgroup? I started with my student resident and her friend. The student was keen on learning group midwifery, and her friend wanted to join until she didn't. Perhaps I was too heavy-handed. We were meeting outside, an unauthorized space, calling ourselves the "nature group" because that sounded innocuous enough and it went along with the image. We would call ourselves something random, because if people knew it was me, or a "helping group," people have funny feelings about being helped. I wanted to develop a subgroup that was capable of empowering other subgroups. To the point, this intergroup was the result of years of Tavistock exploration, and the role of midwifery in groups. My co-worker at the Center for Pastoral Care needed a group, so we became three again.

The NCTS planner stepped out to say hello. Groups were forming and laying claims to authorized spaces. She said, "You really shouldn't be out here, it's disrespectful to the process." To me, this is a very strange interpretation. She was friends with one of the consultants, and that was part of it. But this is not real. This is all a game. We play by some rules for a few hours, and then we decide what it means. Why put up a foul line if fouls are not part of the game? *But they are.* Pro sports could say: "These are the rules; you break the rules you forfeit." But they don't. They say, "Here are the fouls, here are the penalties, manage them as you like. May the best team win." These rules were, "Some spaces are authorized; some are not, don't kill anybody." Okay. I'll keep the body count low. Or, if I don't I'll hide the evidence. I wanted to know what kind of treasure can be found in the space between spaces.

We did some reconnaissance and tried to understand what the different groups were and to anticipate how we might empower them. One group was for "chaplains against Trump," another was for "one-person departments." Some of them were struggling against large cultural problems, some wanted practical encouragement groups, and a couple were focused on questions of meaning as they relate to chaplaincy.

We then created an invitation. With a bold mission statement it read: "Chaplaincy itself is a meaningful response to a world turned upside-down. Please join us in the large room in twenty minutes if you would like to explore this with the other groups." Chaplains have a hard time fitting the system. They usually have a wide range of responsibility: patients, families, staff, anyone passing through, including the man on the road from Jerusalem to Jericho.

Armed with a Xerox, we invited everyone. Sometimes I wonder what Luther could have achieved with a Xerox. Some of the groups came. With the diversity we represented, the three of us facilitated the conversation. The groups were invited to help each other with their own goals, and were invited to consider how their own ministry was a response to the world in distress. We invited them to think about story in a new way, even as they told their own.

Dialogue and story and confession are meaningful responses to a world turned upside down.

A road is a defined concept, but it's really nowhere. You can understand yourself either on it or off it, either between the lines or not. But what the road inherently is remains a space between destinations. People put a lot of energy into demarcating and defending their dearest destinations, but often the roads are left without a guard.

57

I once had a nickname. Nicknames are also given names. I was at a pre-college program back in my high school days. The guys gave me a nickname. "The Lone Biker of the Apocalypse." This is where I really fell in love with Pink Floyd and I was stoked on my sense of alienation.

The nickname was from another movie, *Raising Arizona*. He's a quasi-mythological character; a fiction within a fiction. He is over-the-top in postapocalyptic grunge like from *The Road Warrior*. In a definitive scene, he picks off a fluffy bunny from the horizon with a pistol for target practice. It is beyond silly. There's a similar image in *Ghost Rider* where the hell spawn hero speeds past an innocent lizard on the night plains and it incinerates. Ridiculous.

I took it, like a silly kid in silly high school. It was my high score name for a while, back when people could put their names on the high score screen. And I connected with the name then like I do the "circuit rider" now.

58

The way. The *hodos*. The *logos*. The Tao. The Road.

A well-known quote is, "He who loses the way is lost." That's from the *Tao Te Ching*, which is Chinese for the "Way of Power." *Tao* is Chinese for Way, and the Chinese is as polyvalent as the English or more. Way as in road, path, tradition, even transcendence.

Greek is another polyvalent language. *Logos* is also translated as the way, although in New Testament it has more linguistic connotations. It typically means word or Divine Word.

This was not true for Heraclitus. He is known as Heraclitus the Obscure, but we might better name him Heraclitus the Nondualist, which would also be obscure, since the world loves its extremes and dualisms. For Heraclitus, the term was *Logos*, a term so prominent in my thought that it is as likely to appear in my text without italics as it is with. Which is to say that term is so transcendentally resonant, it is no longer a Greek word, but rather the Word that puts all languages into meaning. The term conveys intelligence, and intelligent design. To borrow from Dylan Thomas, Logos is a word that forks lightning, lightning which Heraclitus says directs all things.

This word is well-known to the Christian reader. When John says, "In the beginning, was the Word," that actual script reads Logos. This word is developed most thoroughly in the Gospel of John, but it occurs throughout the Synoptics as well.

What is less well known is that John has borrowed the term from Heraclitus. "All things proceed from the Word," says Heraclitus. Centuries later, Philo will argue that Heraclitus is borrowing from the time when God spoke, "Let there be," and it was very good. But whether or not Philo is right, Heraclitus introduces the term to the West, not John. His book was left in the Temple of Artemis—goddess of midwives, the same Temple of Ephesus, that John would have visited centuries later.

When Jesus says, "I am the way, the truth, and the life," it is interesting to note that he doesn't use the word *Logos*, not even in John. He uses *hodos*. *Hodos* means street, path, or way. It's the road.

Luke develops this in the book of Acts. Why this euphemism for the early Christian movement only occurs there and then, in Acts, is a question for another day. Of course, it's important to Luke, but how did everybody else miss it? Just to name the hermeneutic, why something is not where it's not has much to do with why it is where it is. It's revealed that the early Christian community is known as "people of the Way." Conflicts were problems with the Way. Those who follow Jesus are said to be followers of the Way.

Chapter 15

The Individual

> The world is twofold
> for man in accordance with his twofold attitude.
> The attitude of man is twofold
> in accordance with the two basic words he can speak.
> The basic words are not single words but word pairs.
> One basic word is the word pair I-You.
>
> **Martin Buber**

> Man's world is manifold, and his attitudes are manifold.
> What is manifold is often frightening because it is not neat and simple.
> Men prefer to forget how many possibilities are open to them.
> They like to be told that there are two worlds and two ways.
> This is comforting because it is so tidy.
> Almost always one way turns out to be common
> and the other is celebrated as superior.
> Those who tell of two ways and praise one
> are recognized as prophets or great teachers.
> They save men from confusion and hard choices.
>
> **Walter Kaufmann**

59

I am not a scholar. There are many things I don't understand, and I don't have time to research. I am a chaplain. I read documents. I have written and read dozens of verbatims. These are the training documents where the chaplain rewrites what was said for peer review. As a CPE educator, I have read hundreds. The rate accelerates by the year.

My favorite documents are what Anton Boisen has named "living, human documents," by which he means the souls of people. I read a lot of those, conceivably thousands, although that is only numerically possible through my group work as a psychiatric chaplain. I read these "living, human documents" as I have learned to read the thousand verbatims; that is, I have learned to read between the lines. Like Evelyn Wood, I have learned to speed-read.

I am going down the hall to meet a student. I bump into another. "I was hoping to bump into you," she says.

"Hi," says I.

"I have this patient, and I don't know what to do. She has three children. Her oldest is in critical condition. He's only seventeen. And she has a twelve-year-old back home, and she's four months pregnant and no one will even come into the hospital to support her. Not even her husband."

"Well, I do not think these children have the same father," I start.

"What?"

"They could, but their ages are too far apart. A teenager and a baby? It does happen, but usually a couple wants their kids closer."

"Oh," she nods. It is a slow "oh," because things from the visit are clicking.

I continue, "The father of the baby may even have complicated feelings about the child of a previous relationship. But that's too hard to say because we can't meet him."

"That's really messy," she says.

"Yes, it is."

You notice a lot of things like this. People reveal secrets they are not ready to confess. That's awkward. Sometimes they realize that I am in the confession with them, that I might have seen too much, and they cut the visit short. This is how I relate to historical figures. I see the gaps in the record, from as many angles as I can, and then I read between the lines. Stories, accounts, and sums are carefully compared and totaled. The figures must match, and my accounting borders obsession. I have my interpretations, but I hold them mercy to the judgment of subsequent data. This is the individual I have become.

60

Has it hit you yet? Our word for the self, "individual," means "that which cannot be divided in two." A house divided cannot stand.

Kaufmann and Buber are trying to tell us the same thing about the human soul, each a reversal of the other. The individual finds awareness in the predicament of being, and the individual is a being that is given this language from the other, and must do all of the thinking in that acquired language, and yet is capable of both new thoughts and new words. The single individual and the society are inseparable as all language must be social. It is a linguistic predicament, predicated on a context of dialogue and dialectic. And from this position, one may communicate and commune. It is this reality that will fall from grace and be named dualism.

Here's an interesting question: is Jesus against Judaism? He is certainly critical of Judaism, but so little of his ministry was extended to the gentiles. In the battle for hearts and minds, the Jews were certainly his focus. For this, Jesus says he has not come to abolish the Law, but fulfill it. But, there was also something undeniably countercultural about his mission. In order to get publicly executed, you have to push against the powers that be, politically, and socially, and Jesus definitely runs afoul of both Jews and Romans.

You can find a very similar dynamic in the ministry of Socrates. At his trial he will be charged with impiety and corrupting the youth. Within time, both of these revolutionary men will become figureheads and symbols of conventional wisdom and established tradition.

It is also meaningful that both of these people went to extreme lengths to redeem the individual. Both of these men took pains, even unto death, to leave the ninety-nine for the sake of the one. The basic paradigm of chaplaincy is an extravagance of resources on behalf of the one, especially for one who is dead.

It is a commentary on the nature of the *status quo*, the dominant culture, and its relationship to reform movements and its own renewal. But it is also keen insight on the relationship between the individual and the group. Thus, it is to explore two questions at once: the question of the individual against the group, and the question of the rebellion against the conventional wisdom (since the latter is almost always how the former plays out). This is an inherent feature of population clusters like New York. There are so many people, the utter fecundity of it—people more populous than piles of rats, that you cannot achieve even the slightest thing without having to overcome the people who stand in your way. Such an environment breeds misanthropy.

I will say it here, and boldly: the individual is the image of God. My work in living, human documents involves the veneration of icons (a scandal to Wesley, I know). These icons are fashioned in blood and tears, and flesh. I stare into the image and see so, so much more.

61

My church got some money together and invited a progressive Methodist to give us a talk. This was in the aftermath of the collapse of the housing market in 2008. The societal pendulum had already swung from the neoconservative patriotism of George Bush and 9/11. I attended the talk because I had finished my project on *Wheelchair Maintenance*, but I struggled with publication for about ten years. The book explores the need for some kind of third way in response to the political dualism of the Left and Right. I attended the talk because at that time progressives were excited about the "way forward" as opposed to a polarized gridlock.

The guest was speaking of the importance of "community." The word felt like it had political import. I asked him about the tension between the individual and the community. I was mortified by what he said next, "I wouldn't actually want to use the word 'individual.'" It was pronounced with disdain in an accent that was more academic than Texan, although it had some of both. Individual had become a dirty word. An obscenity. A vulgarity for stupid people, probably to be coupled and conjoined with the word "rugged." Just to set the tone, Obama had just been elected, and there was meta-chatter around what people could do on their own, and what they ought to do for others. This is when Elizabeth Warren began to argue that the capitalist owed a significant social debt for the benefit of roads and bridges.

It is Kierkegaard who redeems the theology of the individual. And this is why, even though he had his day, he is reduced to a footnote today on his way to being erased. The Platonic Academy will not abide such heresy. The academy must have its collectivism for corralling the masses (so afraid of exile), and its own elite community (so afraid to lose control) to promulgate its gospel. All voices are censored as a means of restricting anything too prophetic. "Scholarship" means consensus of the academic elite, its self-styled philosopher-kings. Should all the people that have ever existed, and all the people that will ever be, attempt to unionize and lock arms and storm the gates of heaven, God would have no problems scattering each and every infinitely far from all else—Kierkegaard reminds us of that. Goodbye faculty lounge.

It is important to understand that there are inherent tensions between the community and the individual. These can bring renewal and invigoration, but they are uncomfortable tensions for those who have to face them.

The community offers safety. It appeals to people who like the safety of numbers. The collectivist is terrified to be alone, like a herd animal in an empty meadow. This terror will always seem irrational to the individual. Thoreau says, "A man thinking or working is always alone, let him be where he will. Solitude is not measured by the miles of space that intervene between a man and his fellows." The group can afford protection because it is so much more powerful than any individual. If I'm a weak person, the group can protect me from strong individuals.

But the dirty secret is that the group can also be overpowered. A lone wolf can drive the herd off the cliff, and some animals hunt that way. In this scenario, the group becomes a weapon of the most broken members of the group. In this context, groups will be resentful and unconsciously oppressive toward powerful individuals. (I think this is in part why society becomes so dangerously uncomfortable when minorities find empowerment—speaking from painful experience.) This is why I am so cautious around big egos. Big egos want to compete through life, and they do not like to lose to the guy in the wheelchair or be passed by. How dare he succeed where they fail? I could have put this in my chapter on the ugly, because people have hostile feelings about the disabled and their children, marriage, career, and things that are widely known as blessings of success.

But the underlying tension between individuals and groups remains accurate and germane to the thread here. Make no mistake: this is what happens with Plato, and why he betrays Socrates so badly. He never forgives the Athenians for the execution of Socrates, and this is why he assembles the academy to overpower the group. Plato's project will go on—and very soon—to empower Alexander the Great to overpower all of Athens. Never mind that Socrates was dedicated to the individual. Plato would rather empower the elite, and seek to control them. Plato must have his revenge.

So, there is bad blood on both sides. Groups have overpowered individuals (Socrates), and individuals (Plato) have overpowered groups. This does not mean that the academics get to declare that "individual" is a dirty word.

Having been exiled and powerless, it is hard to accept what the fuss is all about. Heraclitus says, "Give me one in 10,000 if he be the best." That's at least a hundred times stronger than the good shepherd.

62

A few quotes.
"Resistance to tyranny is obedience to God."

Another: from Marie Durand in the Tower of Constance for thirty-eight years. "Resist." Not spoken, but carved in stone. With her finger.

The next quote is less noble and extended.

> What kind of a man are you? You're worthless and weak! You do nothing! You are nothing! You sit in here all day and play that sick, repulsive, electric twanger! I carried an M16 and you ... you carry that ... that ... that guitar! Who are you? Where do you come from? Are you listening to me? What do you wanna do with your life?"

There is only one answer. "I want to rock."

I watched this video nearly every day before school. This was my morning breakfast. That and *Raiders of the Lost Ark*. What can I say? I drank the Kool-Aid, because I thought it was for kids. Turns out it was this mass-marketed, mass-produced, prediabetic elixir. With poison. And all of this was much harder back then, because you had to wait for it to appear on TV and record it on a blank tape, and then you could watch it over and over. The quotation here is from Twisted Sister, from one of the most famous classic videos of MTV.

There are some interesting notes here. M16s are weapons of Vietnam. Vietnam vets are supposed to be the counterculture generation. What's presented here is that the "dad" in the video is some stuffy conservative. The kid is the wannabe rebel.

These sides switch all the time. This is why dualism is so important for our culture, because it is the essential ingredient for the inversion of the pantheon. The Olympian gods may face mutiny of the titans, but this is only after the Olympian gods themselves have battled and killed the primordial gods.

The weight from the Left is crushing. The weight from the Right is crushing. It doesn't matter which side the previous generation was on, the current generation suffers under the oppression. Maybe the Right has successfully overturned *Roe v. Wade*, maybe they have succeeded in returning to the Constitution of the "Forefathers of the Nation" (this itself is a political slogan that has its own reason for being), but the forefathers themselves were rebels who pushed against centuries of the monarchy.

But this isn't just a jab at traditionalism. The left is equally oppressive. Who dares to speak in this age of cancel culture? And the entire mob of cancel culture can be rallied at a digital whim. And it is so bad that if you don't hate the correct tradition loudly enough you will be torn apart, and destroyed, and never allowed to work again.

Everyone feels this crushing weight, Left or Right. We all want to be free, we all want to rock. We are all rebelling, and rebelling without a clue.

How could we not? The constrained pressure is overwhelming. If there is a way to monetize the fact that everyone feels oppressed, that everyone wants to rebel against this intrusive and oppressive mentality, I am sure that it has been.

Let me just build this out a little further. One navigates the Liar Riddle realizing that one can extract a lie from both, and then just do the opposite of that. What if both sides, Left and Right, are intended to be lies? What is the logical play then? It is one thing to see that the popular media wants to keep us scared; it is another to realize that it wants us to be mindful of how oppressed we are. If we are scared, we can be made to do all kinds of things. We can be made to vote, act, and buy things. With every fiber of our being, we want to break free. Pushing back on this oppression is an involuntary response.

Rebellion. Sin is introduced in the text as the solution to individuation. Given that God is good, and everything created is good, how are we to distinguish and disambiguate ourselves as creation from the Creator? This is what I meant when I mentioned Eve and the burden of being creation. The implied solution is to defy.

Okay. So both the Left and Right are lies, and we want to break free. But what if freedom is found in commitment and surrender? This is what the word "freedom" literally means. How can we find the courage to submit, when the oppressive darkness strangles us at every turn? The true impulse to rock has become weaponized, it has become a thing that holds us in bondage, and makes us to do that which we don't want. We yearn to say, "Yes," to God, all the while Satan enters stage left, grinning, "I bet I can make you say, 'no.'" It is hard to embrace submission and surrender when one feels the weight of oppression at every turn. Do you feel the fear that is preached from every pulpit? Do you taste the dust in the back of your throat? Do you feel the constricting spirit at every turn?

The task is to become oneself. To become what was created to be. To allow that to happen and to ignore all the noise even if the noise is screaming at you, in your face. To push forward without pushing back. I remember a T-shirt that had the image of a rocking angel and on the back: "Reborn to be wild!"

CHAPTER 16

The Midwife

Even when the transition is understood, it is of surprising power.
The birthgiver is gripped by tremendous force
and feels that she has somehow lost control.
Everything is suddenly too big and too powerful.
All the weeks of careful preparation and instruction
seem inadequate and trivial.
The birthgiver had thought she was prepared
and "knew just what to do"
—and now it doesn't work!
She might even feel betrayed:
no one has told her the truth,
or perhaps no one has previously confronted and understood the truth.

MARGARET GUENTHER

63

There are many stories about midwifery, so many that it becomes overwhelmingly hard to talk about. There are many ways to introduce it. I could tell the story of how I stumbled on it. I could tell the story of how it lies within history, and how its ideas grew. There's how I wrote my book on midwifery, and the rationale for why the book is laid out that way. There's the story about how the practice has played a role in my life, defined my ministry, and given me focus. I could tell how it has made sense of my past, gives me the pathway for the future, and guides me in the present moment. I don't think the way to introduce it is to showcase it with an example, because as a tradition, it has a way of being overlooked and misunderstood. You could stare right at it and not know what you were looking at unless you already knew what to look for.

I have been searching for the Holy Grail since 1978 or so. I was six. Warren Robinett created a game for the Atari, and the quest was to return the chalice to the Gold Castle. It is a game that I played for years of my life. I had no idea what chalices were, or how inspired he was by mythology and fantasy. I had no idea how his game would eventually turn into the gnostic movie *Ready Player One*.

I confess that I have said to my favorite students that spiritual midwifery is the "holy grail" of pastoral care. When I usually make this kind of disclosure, I mean it more than one way. It wouldn't be me if there weren't some kind of "dad joke" in it. When I say it is the "holy grail," in a very vernacular sense I mean simply that it is cool in the superlative sense. It is the coolest thing I have ever found in the study of pastoral care.

It is also a way of doing pastoral care—a value system—that we find in the Gospels, the very method of Jesus. But we also find a footnote. The tradition is absolutely emphatic that Jesus prayed that "God would take the cup away" just prior to the crucifixion. I'll amplify that, because Jesus was alone in those prayers so therefore Jesus alone is responsible for that part of the tradition. If no one else was there, he had to tell that in a report to a witness. My argument is that we use metaphors that are meaningful. It doesn't make sense to make an allusion or a reference if people don't catch the referent. Right? But at that point in history, there was only one famous public execution involving a cup. That would be the execution of Socrates. The Jews used stones (as with my namesake). Only the Greeks used poison cups. I think it's completely likely that in a Hellenized Judaica that Jesus would know about Socrates, and it makes me smile because Socrates coins "spiritual midwife" and his dialogues helped me understand the parables. So: "holy grail." But this is the grail he drank from, not necessarily the one that caught his blood.

Here is another confession. We know about dealing with the devil. It is also true that we bargain with God. We pray for things and in the unfolding of life and reality the prayer is answered. As we pray, we put in terms and conditions. It's probably a really dangerous spiritual practice, but invariably we all find ways of putting fleece before the Lord.

At one point, I was being surpassed in my career by someone I had helped and who had started later than I did. I was bitter. You work really hard and you can't make the progress you want as easily as others do. I made peace through prayer and a bargain. The bargain was, "If my career doesn't advance, so be it, but please teach me about the soul."

This Solomon's wisdom has been spiritual midwifery. Not only have I learned about the soul, but the focus has saved my soul, and more than once.

The phrase comes from Plato's *Theaetetus*. It is the name Socrates takes for himself. The pericope seems to be so unabashedly within the Heraclitus tradition, and Artemis, that it is really perpendicular to Plato's Parmenides project, and it sounds like a piece of hidden truth. Kind of in the same way Gospel scholars believe sayings of Jesus especially if they are difficult for the early Christian community.

I did my initial research and writing into midwifery in 2000. It turned into a published text in 2014, and I wrote the text in a very philosophical way because at the time, I thought it might get to be the last thing I ever wrote on the subject. In more depth, there is a rhetorical and philosophical history there that was very much a part of how I came to understand midwifery at all. And I do think those philosophical ideas illuminate much of the underlying value system on which midwifery is built. However, some students have turned away from midwifery due to what are essentially flaws and limitations of my own presentation. Simply, you don't have to follow all of my ideas and convoluted language to get it.

What spiritual midwifery is: an applied and specific use of consciousness on behalf of another. However, because it is a use of consciousness, and because we are consciousness, proficiency in midwifery means that you have to become something. To learn it requires a willingness to be transformed. And because it is targeted on behalf of another, there is no room for big egos. That's hard for many readers, much harder than my inadequacy in philosophical explication. But the good news is: the best predictor in whether or not someone really grasps the methodology is that this learning is a function of desire. If you really want it, you're going to get it.

Why is it called "midwifery"? Because that's what I found. It is a found methodology. It is not because I think there is something marketable or "edgy" by incorporating a feminine metaphor (regardless of the fact that I am fond of feminine images and metaphors). It is simply because it is found, and the people who used it or more broadly the traditions where I have found it have called it midwifery.

John's Gospel, that is John of Ephesus, will use the midwifery image again with Jesus and Nicodemus. Socrates goes out of his way to define the role of the midwife, but John's exposition on the mother and baby was no less fascinating. This echo, some five centuries later, inspired me to use Platonic dialogues to dissect and map the parables of Jesus, both for applications in my own pastoral care and my own spiritual practices. I have never been the same.

64

There are two defining energies of the chaplain: male and female. After my many years, I am surprised to cast these words in such an engendered way. You would think we could describe this in a Platonic form. But chaplaincy is about engaging the spirituality of living people, and living people find themselves engendered. It's been easy to talk about the male energy because that's as easy as talking about myself. I think the male archetype is that of the survivalist sojourner. In the Moses tradition that's the archetype of the liberator.

I can get into trouble for writing anything about the female energy. I can be accused, and have been, of appropriating women's territory. Of course, neither Jesus nor Socrates were deterred from this imagery. They did not see it as beneath them, nor was it so high above them that they refused to use it. As men themselves, I think the embodied paradox necessitated that they use this metaphor, because nothing screams transcendence like paradox.

If the male energy of the chaplain is the survivalist sojourner, the female energy is the midwife. The chaplain has both. The male travels far and finds a new land, the female stays still and finds new life. The male journeys without, the female journeys within.

Every metaphor has a vehicle and tenor. That is to say, every metaphor has an ironic resonance in the dialectic between its vehicle and tenor. Every metaphor has an image and has a meaning. Every metaphor is a balance between form and content.

Technically, there are two vehicles. There is the vehicle of the midwife: the individual that is in the exclusive role; and, there is the vehicle of the midwifery: the surrounding art of the dynamism between mother and baby and thereunto the helper that has been assigned.

The first vehicle is the role, although you can never entirely define the midwife without occasional reference to midwifery—admittedly it is a circular explanation. But as a vehicle, I have long admired that midwifery is the last clinical posture that is not oriented toward pathology. That is, most clinical postures are oriented toward disease. Midwifery is oriented to a healthy and natural process. It is a process of generativity and vitality. A process that occurs when things are going well. And yet, the posture remains clinical.

The midwife is a "helping third." The chief business occurs within the mother-baby dyad. The midwife is located outside that dyad for the purpose of helping. The helping third is preferred, but not necessary. It is optional. Women are amazing beings and they are capable of giving birth unassisted, although birth has its own dangers and there are lives in the balance, and it's just plain hard, and so many of them will prefer to have the assistance where possible.

I can say a lot about the vehicle of the midwife. At the risk of shifting over to the tenor too soon, and in a real sense, it is all I ever talk about, so the challenge is to say enough to be useful without overwhelming the reader with new information. There are tips and traits, but it is deceptive to think that the midwife is the tips and traits. That all one has to do is mimic the tips and traits, and, *voila,* one is doing midwifery. Not so fast; more than anything else a midwife is a commitment to a very intense process. A bit further, it is a commitment that will result in changing everyone involved, including the midwife herself.

One of the most helpful things in describing the midwife is to know that she receives an inverted authority. She is granted access to the mother because of her skill and experience, in short, her expertise, like any other trained clinician. But she attends the mother at the lowly place, the vulnerable place, neither vaulted nor vaunted. Only the trusted are permitted there, but it's no place for the proud. To put it bluntly, the midwife can expect to get pooped on. For in one poem what might be "the old high way of love" will be in another "the place of excrement," ironically even by the same poet. This is the inverted authority. Authority is conferred to be humble.

The other vehicle is midwifery proper. This is birthing.

This is the work between mother and baby, and by far, this is the main event. What happens here is far and away more important than anything related to the midwife. This is the reason for being. The work of the mother is the only work that matters.

While we have touched on the fact that Socrates and Jesus are men, and paradoxically so, there is another paradox between mother and baby, the resolution of which was lost on Nicodemus, who could only envision a solution by reclaiming the lost territory of his mother's womb. The paradox is that the one doing the hard work (the mother) is also the beneficiary of the hard work. That is, the individual alone benefits from being born again. Thus, the tenor of this metaphor is also a paradox: mother and baby are essentially one.

This does not mean that the Divine is excluded. As we move back and forth between vehicle and tenor, the one that is ultimately responsible for the new life is neither the midwife, nor even the mother, but only the Divine.

Another thing about the tenor, as it relates to the vehicle of general midwifery: there are certain things where people benefit from help. One is learning how to swim, which is essentially a relearning of our uterine experience. But the conscious mind struggles to remember before drowning, and so a guide is helpful. A second, as discussed, is birthing. A third is the spiritual life, which is enhanced by an external point of view, and this is the need for clergy in general and chaplains in particular. It is normal. Like women who birth alone, there are mystics and spiritual geniuses who figure it out. But they are rare. Clergy are natural and useful, although this is undermined by the fact that the corruption of clergy is common.

65

This brings to the surface the problem of what is and what is not spiritual midwifery. Nobody owns the term. Birth and rebirth have been metaphors for the spiritual life for thousands of years. Birth itself is holy, since that is, in fact, how we all get here.

So, a lot of people like to claim the term *spiritual midwifery*. The CPSP refers to midwifery in a very general way, but they don't define it and they don't work with the history of it. And they weren't nearly as excited as I have been by my writing and research.

Many people who work in spirituality and religion talk about rebirth and midwifery. But they don't really have an idea in mind, or a theory. It's a sexy term, and there are midwives in the Bible, and "spiritual midwifery" can become as meaningless as "ministry of presence."

A few words about what passes for ministry in the name of "ministry of presence." If chased into a corner most people would confess that what the really mean is "nonverbal, passive ministry support" and that this type of ministry is best employed in extended emergency settings. Or something like that. The very fact that they can't name it should scare the pants off of everyone.

The biggest problem is that it is passed on as an aphoristic shibboleth. Somebody begins training and they feel overwhelmed by their own experience of the hospital encounter. The newbies ingratiate themselves to the veterans, and with saucer eyes they stammer, "How do you do it? How do you go in there?" They nod with the affectation of gravitas, "Ministry of presence," they gravel.

One season later, the former newbies have progressed nicely through their first unit exposure therapy. When the next crop of newbies appears with an all-too-familiar terror and they are delighted to act like they know something. They now get to use the clichés that were handed to them. And the newcomers cry, "How do you do this?" And they think they know what the cliché means simply because they themselves are no longer spooked by a trauma room.

What I'm trying to caricature is not that people are new. I pray that there are always new people. I'm trying to caricature how aphoristic transmission happens. How clichés without understanding replace comprehension in pedagogy. This is aphoristic transmission at best. This is not theory.

When pastoral care practice becomes an aphorism, this is not training. It's certainly not theology. It's a shibboleth that sifts the anxious from the non-anxious and that's about it.

Not only is this incredibly paltry and watered down (with intended echoes of biblical scorn for lukewarm water), but it becomes anti-theory. It becomes theory that now means the opposite of what it was meant to mean, but nobody knows or cares because all the shibboleths and aphorisms have all been pronounced correctly. And yes, the keepers of tradition have been lousy guards.

To the point, "ministry of presence" was inspired genius from the pen of Henri Nouwen, one of Boisen's early followers. And what he meant was, you don't have to have an academic answer for the person in pain. You don't have to fill the air with nervous chatter, prattle, and preaching. You can actually operate out of a contemplative practice and learn how to serve with other dimensions of yourself than your tongue. Absolutely right.

Instead, we have self-satisfied clergy who think that showing up and smiling at patients makes them better. Behind a toothy grin, "ministry of presence!" As if that was what it was. The ministry of presence is not cheering them up or keeping them company. Chaplaincy is not the art of making good cheer. One of my colleagues was right when he said therapy dogs do that. It is this kind of backwards thinking that confuses the art of pastoral care with exhorting them to practice self-care. Admonishment to brush their teeth, or anything else, is not the same as providing spiritual care in their hour of need. Said differently, telling people to take obvious care of themselves is no substitute for the spiritual care provided by a professional.

People become convicted by ministry of presence because it's a jargon that justifies not knowing what to do. That's a basic existential crisis, and who wouldn't prefer a buzzword over an existential crisis?

Sometimes this is hidden in a theological gloss, and this happens when ministry of presence is consecrated as "incarnational." That's not an idea, that's an ad slogan, if you can't articulate how this incarnational theology actually works, what its parts are, and how they actually fit together—i.e., show me the theory. Where, pray tell, oh incarnated chaplain, is your crucifixion and resurrection? And how is your incarnation any different from the incarnation of anyone on the multidisciplinary team? Is incarnation simply having a body? I won't believe it until you show me the nails, and I touch them with my own fingers. From this end, ministry of presence under the guise of incarnational theology is hiding the lack of a solid theory behind a holy mystery.

This is what happens when we rely on aphorisms and clichés instead of real theory. What we create are people who can speak the jargon, not chaplains who can think theologically. Inverted ministry of presence, in the colloquial rite not named by Nouwen, is for Santa Claus. As for me and my house, we will have some "ministry of absence."

66

I have tried to say elsewhere what is spiritual midwifery. In just a few words, I would describe "spiritual midwifery" as a set of values that are extrapolated from reverse engineering the parables. It takes a certain kind of mindset and rhetorical technology to engineer the parables. The parables create a literary transcendence for those who "have ears to hear." Through hearing the parables a transcendence emerges that bypasses that dualism that obstructs the spiritual life. This dualism may also be termed *resistance*.

Once you begin to see the accompanying values that make spiritual midwifery possible, you can exercise the values without limiting yourself to parables only. One value is "empowerment through submission." There are many. Another value is the super-importance of the spiritual life.

I have tried to lay out some of its history, and provide some language for its aspects that are most counterintuitive, although it is debatable if I have confused an already confusing topic.

What I have not committed to writing is how I try to teach the midwifery. What follows are a series of questions directed to students as they reflect on their chaplain-patient encounters.

1. *How did the patient's belief system affect your relationship? Did they trust you? Dismiss you? Underestimate you? How did they understand you? What kinds of things did they project onto you and did that help or hinder?*

The chaplain must learn that all of the emerging data is a dynamic product of the chaplain-patient dynamic. What the patient thinks about clergy, chaplains, religion, the chaplain's demographic markers will highly inform what is possible for the relationship. This is learning the art of "mutual assessment" because a simultaneous and bidirectional assessment is unfolding. The observer and subject interpenetrate. Someone of the same race, gender, or religion of the patient is likely going to have a completely different encounter. This contrasts to the Newtonian view, that the patient has a singular diagnosis, and that any "interfaith spiritual caregiver" could meet that need. This is built on the belief that the "work" that emerges between the chaplain and patient is unique to that relationship, and there is not one and only one "work" that helps the patient grow. In the data analysis, the chaplain's demographics matter. Much of the surrounding conversation balks at the idea that there is identifiable work.

"Work" is not code for "psychotherapeutic issue." Work, instead, resonates with the labor of birthing. A lot of colleagues resist the concept of work, because the assertion of the existence of work also asserts the horror of judgment for the chaplain. You might miss the work; it is the specter of failure and this specter is denied by people who think being gregarious and extroverted is chaplaincy.

For the record, there is not one and only one work. There are many psalms and there are many expressions and responses toward God. While this is true, most people are capable of holding one—possibly two—dominant responses toward God at a time. Even a psalm that has several distinct moods toward God relies on distinction between each to create a sense of movement and trajectory. The possible work that emerges will be based on what this particular chaplain-patient relationship may bear. The individuality of the chaplain and the individuality of the patient will intersect in a unique way, creating a field where some conversational avenues are more auspicious than others.

2. *What was their dominant response to God? Given the totality of your assessment, what was the major need? If the patient doesn't believe in God, what is preventing them from moving forward in life?*

The spiritual life is a long journey of individual steps. Each individual step is an expression of the dominant response to God. These expressions are statements, actions, silences, prayers, and tears. The dialogue with the chaplain is overlain with a much more expansive dialogue with God. It often happens that the dominant response to God has been the most problematic and it has emerged because the patient has assessed the presence of a capable helper.

For example, the psalms often create movement through the sequential transition of the expression of one dominant response to God to the next. There are many responses but for the most part they are experienced one at a time. Too many, and the collective experience is singular overwhelm.

It is in this area where a lot of spiritual midwifery becomes recognizable and distinct from other ways of being. Because the "dominant response to God" is thought to be spontaneous, a lot of consideration is given toward resistance. In my book of the same name, I joke that midwifery could have been better packaged and sold as RBT, or resistance-based therapy. While there are many possibilities, they are aspirational toward the uninhibited expression from within as opposed to some kind of teaching or directive that the chaplain might offer from without.

3. *Where is the complication in the response (were they angry, for example, but afraid of anger toward God; or, angry at men and the chaplain is male)?*

Students love to say there is no complication, and that everything exactly is as it is presented at face value. This is silly, and if people didn't need help in the spiritual life professional clergy would not exist. The complication can lie between competing values, conflicts with God, decision-making and dilemmas, traditions, and even interpersonally between the chaplain and patient.

4. *What was your plan to help this response? How did that go?*

Most students try to dodge this, too, saying, "I didn't want to walk in there with an agenda." The question assumes that the chaplain has to begin to come up with a dominant response to God. Yes, good for you, you didn't have an agenda. Your job is to go in and find one. The chaplain must then attempt to support the expression of that response that anticipates the complexities of surrounding complications. The chaplain then is asked to evaluate effectiveness, in the hopes of doing better next time. Not only do we have to see and understand who this human being is, but we have to interact with them in a helpful way despite surrounding complications. The alternative is "tell me what I'm supposed to do for you." This question is about training the mind for clinical and critical thinking in the next pastoral encounter.

67

There is a common fear that people have when they begin to really understand midwifery. It is the fear of being alone.

Part of the fear stems from an underlying misunderstanding about the nature of intimacy and bonding. Since the metaphor of midwifery returns to very intimate aspects of our humanity and personhood, it would be good to revisit.

Most people think they have arrived at intimacy because they have shared an experience with someone. We both find something at the same time, and we believe that the shared something now binds us together. This touches on the trust that people place in things that are found, as opposed to things that are presented. This is an unconscious and inexperienced way of engaging the world. This happens in families of siblings; we find ourselves in the predicament of the same household. Or it happens in classrooms; students all endure the same inept teacher. Or it happens as young people discover sexuality. In the arms of another, perhaps even despite any differences of gender, they discover very personal things about themselves, along with someone who is making very parallel discoveries.

This is the intimacy of fusion. We are fused together because we have experienced the same thing at the same time and now we are fused into one. It is a regressive fantasy probably stemming from wanting to fuse with the mother. Baby may experience this intimacy as unity, as utter oneness, but this is a misunderstanding. Mother too experiences intimacy but she experiences this intimacy as reciprocal and complementary, *not identical and parallel*. Mother has a much different headspace than baby. She will mediate and manage the entire world for him; for him, she is the entire world. This is called reciprocal bonding.

People who think that intimacy is essentially and only fusion often reject the idea of spiritual midwifery in the name of "ministry of presence," although such a posture suggests that they don't even know the history of "ministry of presence." They will resist really engaging the patient "because they only just met" and "they haven't earned the right to talk about real things." When the baby is crowning, mother doesn't care if the midwife just got there. These kind of chaplains criticize the midwife as being "inauthentic" and disingenuous. As being dishonest. Their paradigm is flawed; honesty comes from what is chosen and committed to, not what is found. Do you really think Jesus experienced the parables the same way as his audience? But are they not Scripture because they are the truest things ever said? A student recently confessed that she had learned parables were "manipulative." I loved that word in this context. Yes, midwives can perform manipulations of mother and baby when they need to.

No matter what, you don't want to have parallel and identical experience of bonding with your oncologist. You don't want to discover the same tumor in your body with newfound wonder. You don't want to hear, "Wow, I've never seen a tumor like that before." You want the oncologist to be very bored, knowing exactly what to do because they have seen it all a million times. The mother does not want to be there when the midwife discovers the beauty of the female body for the first time.

Fusion is how people connect when they are immature and unconscious in their bonding. It becomes idealized, but it is a barrier to the professional intimacy that reciprocal bonding requires. The roles of midwife and mother require mutually exclusive responsibility. Fusion comes into chaplaincy when both parties have a sloppy conversation with poor boundaries, stay friends forever, and cry together with exactly the same tears for the same reason. The fusion-oriented chaplain will struggle with setting limits, saying goodbye, being misunderstood, ending visits on time, and most of all saying "no." They trusted me, they will argue with themselves, how can I disappoint them? As if the most basic professional boundary would violate intimacy and breech sacred trust.

Maybe spirituality is a very intimate subject for the patient. Maybe the patient has only ever spoken of God with his pastor or his lover. That does nothing to change the fact that the chaplain has these conversations all the time, and does so for a living. Just because the intimacy is different for both parties does not mean that the midwife is not vulnerable. Or unchanged. Indeed, both parties are changed forever.

What is really at work here is that the fusion-oriented chaplain is afraid of being alone. Afraid of being an individual before God. If everyone else does relationships based on fusion, and I connect differently, what will happen to me? Who will meet my unmet needs? It's a fair question, but it is unfair to expect those under your care to provide the answer.

How is anyone alone? I am easily amused by words. I look at the word "midwife." It is not "quasi-wife," like "half-wife." It is "mid" as "in the midst of." It seems to me a nice, nondualist expression for what is a nondualist art. One is surrounded by wifery on all sides. Like the center of an infinite circle, like the cosmos itself.

CHAPTER 17

The Question

You are free and that is why you are lost.

KAFKA

68

It was an interview. I was there at the Center for Pastoral Care, just outside Trenton, New Jersey. There was nothing special about the day. It was cold, so he pulled up his coat and sat. Each year, we go through several rounds of interviews, both for the internships offered there and for the residency. I teach CPE. CPE stands for Clinical Pastoral Education, and this is the pastoral care training process for many religious denominations, and it is essential for credentialing as a professional chaplain.

CPE internship interviews are very strange, because they are unlike any other interview process. You are not looking for skilled service providers. (This is probably much to the horror of any hospital administrator that might turn these pages.) You are, by definition, looking for people that are untrained. And you are looking for people that are trainable. In CPE, that means people who are capable and willing to explore themselves, regardless of who or what they might discover.

This is harder than it sounds. How would an applicant actually know if they were ready for the training—or even if they wanted it at all—if they did not know themselves? The riddle is not: is the applicant deceiving the interviewer; but rather, is the applicant deceiving themself? So you sit down, and you talk together, and you try to figure out if the training can happen. The interview begins, and you ask your questions.

And then the applicant has their questions.

I am deeply committed to the ideals of dialogue. And a training relationship is a very special dialogue. If I am going to ask you to explore yourself, and many other things, then the spirit of equanimity needs room for a question or two. It's only fair for you to be able to ask your own question. So, I invited it.

He asked, "What is it that keeps you coming back?"

I became very uncomfortable.

Another supervisor might have said: "Well, it is hard to come back every day. Things happen in hospitals. So, you go home and refuel and recharge. You have boundaries and self-care, Sunday worship. This is why I still enjoy pastoring and preaching every Sunday. It's good for the soul. But it is rewarding to help the patients. And it is even more rewarding to train and equip future leaders of the church. You get to make a mark on the future."

I answered.

I do not understand your question. Your question does not make sense to me. It is confounding and backwards.

The question implies that I am going somewhere under duress. That I am going somewhere I do not wish to go. That I am going somewhere unbearable. And once in such a place, that I would retreat from it. Maybe return home. Bandage wounds. Recover. Rest. Heal.

No. This is not my story. I am not going somewhere under duress. I am not going somewhere that I do not wish to go. I am not compelled to go anywhere. And yet there is a peculiar calling on my life that has never, ever stopped.

Stranger still is the notion that I could ever arrive anywhere on this journey. How could I go back to a place where I have never been? "Here" and "there" need each other. They follow each other. They define each other. Can you have a "here" if there is no "there"? And if you do not have a "there" nor a "here" how can you possibly go back? Where are we trying to get to? How can we think about going back if we don't know where we are going? *This is a journey.*

I have been so far. You can't speak of it in miles. Tears would be closer, but even the tears have stopped. Life is dearly sweet, and dearly short. It is intense like the sun. From birth to death I have seen so much. Too much. I'm not who I was. He is gone.

Coming back? I have no expectation of surviving this. I'm not getting out of this alive. I'm not going to make it. And that's a very good thing. They're not going to find the body.

But it makes me think of working with addicts in recovery. And if they are working with me, that means recovery has failed, because I only find the failures, and their lives have been completely so. They have burned each and every bridge, betrayed each and every beloved. But somewhere on this road to ruin, they have found a Higher Power. Sometimes with a little encouragement, but usually without, the addicts will get philosophical. They will surmise that had they never taken the path of perdition they would have never found their Higher Power. And then, with a profound wisdom, the kind of wisdom that knows the utmost is bought at any price—always at a bargain, they count themselves blessed.

I'm not coming back.

CHAPTER 18

The Fire

*That which always was, and is, and will be
Everliving fire,
The same for all, the cosmos, made neither by god nor man,
Replenishes in measure as it burns away.*

*Fire in its ways of changing
is a sea transfigured
between forks of lightning and the solid earth.*

*As all things change to fire,
and fire exhausted falls back into things,
the crops are sold for money spent on food.*

The lightning directs all things.

HERACLITUS

69

This is a meditation on the mutability of fire. This is my alchemical chapter. I have always been intrigued by this aforementioned quote of Heraclitus: "The One, the only wisdom, does and yet does not consent to be called Zeus." I've always read this as a reflection of the hidden nature of God's name. Elsewhere, Heraclitus says, "Things keep their secrets." That sounds about right.

But what if it means something else entirely? What if it means, or also means, you really can call God Zeus, and that doing so would work both for you and for God just fine? That God likes being called Zeus, at least as much as God likes being called anything? What does it matter what word we use? I have heard Heraclitus indicting the presumptuousness of humanity, but what if he also highlights ambivalence in God?

To the point, if the cry is hallelujah, how do we know if it is the holy or the broken hallelujah?

70

Keeping the fire going is important.

For years, I have been moved by the idea of the sacred fire. Perhaps to the reader this reveals signs of a sub-diagnosed bipolar depression. That at times, I am definitely unstoppable, and at other times, I definitely can't get going. The difference between the two is the sacred fire.

I think this is true for healthcare workers and true of ministry, and possibly doubly true for hospital chaplains. When you constantly tend the sick, the cheerful bunch that they are, you never really see wellness. Think about it. During those years when I was doing the Center for Pastoral Care, I would often wear neckties with images of lightning or flames; either abstractly representative or pictorial.

Not for nothing, my own Methodist denomination has latched onto this symbol in a way that defies the culture. Our symbol is the "Cross and Flame." With all of the Southern churches, and all of the cross burnings, I'm surprised that it hasn't been changed. But theologically, my denomination is remarkably committed to the doctrine of the Holy Spirit, which was encountered fifty days after the resurrection at Pentecost. Wesleyan spirituality has a lot to do with the establishment of Pentecostalism and other churches in the Holiness movement.

71

So what is the fire anyway?

Is it the Zoroastrian purity flame of the fire temples?

Is the Divine Spirit like a fire? That's what Heraclitus seems to say.

Is the Divine Spirit like a woman of wisdom? I'm referring to the Sophia tradition from Proverbs.

Is this fire some strange power of language, that is uniquely tied to Pentecost and the upper room?

Is the great fire the burning sun?

Is the fire demonic? The fires of hell? The Light Bearer? Lucifer?

Is it the "refiner's fire" of Job, Isaiah, Malachi, and Peter?

Is the fire the ingenuity of Vulcan, or the arrogance of Prometheus and Icarus?

Is fire the burning bush? Is it John the Baptist who proclaims Jesus will baptize in the Holy Spirit and fire?

Is it that fluid? Is it that mutable?

This is closely related to what we have said about fairy tales. The made-up stories become the truth. Meanings, symbols, and narratives are deliberately inverted. You can bank on this: the swastika meant something different when the Germans chased it down in Tibet. It is a war of logos and advertising, and actual history is much less potent than branding.

Words invert. Meanings are superimposed and swapped. This is intentional. Confusion is planted. If our country "sanctions" Iran, does that mean we prohibit or condone Iran?

Today's academic student is not given a contextual definition of "capitalism." Capitalism is about free will and the fair exchange of goods or services. How many fish is your bag of grain worth? Let's bargain. Capitalism breaks down when the exchange is no longer fair. The big corporations lobby Congress to have so much compliance regulation that small companies can't compete. This is an abuse of socialism that is termed "corporate capitalism" and the young student is taught that Marx is the answer. To really spell out the socialism, the "elite" who cannot create or compete in the marketplace seek to dominate the individual by manipulating the collective government. We did not need to invert the term "capitalism" to describe this evil. We already had the language of the "seven deadly sins" and this amply qualifies as "greed." But we can outgrow and abolish the seven deadly sins and say that we are beyond sin, all the while we continue to lobby Congress to change the rules for political and financial gain. I write for an educated audience, and this is the most scandalous paragraph in the book. This is the paragraph that takes everyone's sacred cow to the Fourth of July cookout. I don't mean to suggest that capitalism is perfect. As an expression of free will it is prone to corruption, and especially the corruption of stealing the free will of others. When your only qualification for the degrading experience called a "job" is that you are otherwise too poor to decline, that is, by any logic, exploitation.

But "alchemical" suggests a process that can go two ways. Light can change into shadow, but it can be made clear again. Remember that. So, yes, we can invert and pervert language all the time, and we will continue to do this in measure to the perversion within. Thoreau has a hilarious line about this. He says that we pursue comfort and warmth to keep the fire from going out, but we get so entangled in our material wealth and privilege that we are kept unnaturally hot; indeed cooked "*a la mode*."

But, yes, God is still speaking and capable of being revealed everywhere, even in the lies from yesterday.

72

Woodburning is something I enjoy. I started doing it in Boy Scouts, probably forty years ago. And I would be surprised if it is something I have done more than forty times. There are reasons for this. The process is difficult, and it is largely a summer activity. There is some eyestrain. There is often sunburn.

There are fancy kits. I even bought one once, and with the fancy kits you get an electric tool hot enough that it burns the wood where you touch it. One of my burnings was made this way, and I burned myself several times because I don't really know how to use it, and I only did it once. I can't do anything well once.

The preferred method is to get a nice piece of wood, and get a simple image on it in a dark marker like purple or blue. Brown or black becomes indistinguishable from the burn portions and you can't tell what has been burned from what is yet to be burned. You then get a magnifying glass. And when the sky is clear and not hazy, and when the sun is directly overhead, you go out. You focus the sun into an even brighter small dot—this is the eyestrain—and you follow the image on the wood. For shading, I smudge the ashes with my finger. The noon sun is not necessary; I've done a couple in the winter, but at different times in the day you have to work your glass at odd angles and this leads to muscle cramping and soreness.

I usually leave them unvarnished. If you stain them, the ashes smudge badly. It is a simple process and oddly satisfying. When it starts to burn, it goes very fast. It's not like cooking the wood; it's like art with a high-powered laser. As you trace the drawing, and you move things around you have to recapture the focal point. It doesn't take much of a glass. Even a weaker glass at double magnification can start a fire. Yes, the sun is that big.

For me, the art is the whole thing. The whole process. So I don't see it as a test of my drawing skills. I spent many hours drawing as a kid and never got very good. My disability was too much to overcome. In 1986, there were no drawing programs, and I even wrote one for the Apple IIe, which predated the Macintosh computer. Just saying, I spent a lot of time thinking about images. The screen resolution was something like 272 x 191. That was hi-res. Lo-res was a pitiful 40 x 40. My program allowed me to draw dot by dot. In many ways, I have lived dot by dot. Anyway, I don't constrain myself regarding how I get the image onto the wood. There's no such thing as cheating. I have done free hand, but I have also measured points with a ruler, and then connected the dots. Tracing is perfectly acceptable, because the goal is the end product. Tracing is hard, though, and usually this means scoring it with a ballpoint pen, and then going over those lines with a marker.

The last difficulty is that the burning happens fast. Once it's focused, it is burning. You are drawing with the sun itself. Thus, it is very, very easy to make mistakes. Imperfections get into the work very easily. And then they either have to be incorporated or the work is rejected. My kids have very steady hands, but I don't. And for me it's "hand," for the record.

My favorite image is a rendition of the labyrinth from Chartres Cathedral. This labyrinth itself is a famous Christian image. Pilgrims would come for miles to walk this walking meditation on the floor of the cathedral. Lauren Artress has popularized the labyrinth project the world over. It is absolutely not a maze designed to confound; there is only one path that leads the pilgrim to the holy center.

I once saw an image of the Chartres labyrinth that was superimposed by the image on the yin-yang, an image adopted by the early Taoist religion as a sign of nondualism. I loved it. For my concept, I had to use a simpler labyrinth because Chartres has eleven circuits, meaning you have to go through eleven levels to get to the center. Yes, this is another *entendre* of "circuit rider." The magnifying focal point is about as wide as a fat-tipped marker so if you need something that detailed, you're going to need a really big piece of wood. I used a model with eight circuits that are often mistaken for the Chartres. The concept was that with the "black" side, the labyrinth path, would be burned, and then on the "white" side it would be left unburned. This is, of course, except for the two dots where everything is inverted.

I sat with the kids on a dock, overlooking Lake Owassa in New Jersey. After hours of planning, it was done in about forty-five minutes. It is something akin to the meditative practice of performing calligraphy in water. It is something that takes place in time, and what you end up with is what you end up with.

I love it.

73

Is the answer with Heraclitus or Parmenides?

I haven't quoted Parmenides once, and the reader knows I can't keep myself from quoting Heraclitus. Much of my favoritism comes from the role of Heraclitus in helping me understand the Logos, dialogue, dialectic, and the underlying philosophical history of midwifery. This also pulls in ideas and mythologies about the feminine, Artemis, Ephesus, and the Gospel according to John.

Plato has a lot to do with how these thinkers were introduced to me. Virtually no credit is given to Heraclitus whose disciple is criticized, and Parmenides is set out as the teacher of Socrates. Sometimes I don't explicate this enough, because it's like talking about family members—all of the historical drama is fused with my inner life and I take for granted what the reader knows and doesn't. So, with a wry smile, and like the man says, "From the beginning . . ."

Plato's highest idea is the Forms, through which he crowns his philosopher-kings. Plato credits the Forms to Parmenides who by any reckoning sings antiphonal to Heraclitus. Moreover, Plato seems to discredit Heraclitus at every opportunity (and through that heuristic we can carve out Socratic thought). So, it's easy to take Heraclitus/Parmenides as a contrasting pair, and Heraclitus/Cyrus-Darius as a contrasting pair. I smile at myself because contrast itself is how we wedge dialectic to pry understanding from our unconsciousness.

But this becomes remarkably simplistic, and we are convicted by Kaufmann's indictment: "*our ways are manifold.*"

Have you seen Parmenides' poem? It's beautiful. And there are many lines that capture my imagination. The poem is called "On Nature." It is purported that Heraclitus's surviving fragments (this alone is worth the aside to wonder why this man who was so important to Darius the Great was almost completely erased from history) don't come from a book "Fragments," but that they also come from a work called, "On Nature." What are the odds? Maybe we will never know who spoke first, or who was more influenced by Zarathustra, but these men are clearly talking to each other. In the poem of Parmenides, we find ourselves at the feet of the goddess Night, who stands guard of the dualism between day and night. A goddess guarding dualism itself. She says, "Traveler, there are two roads, the Way of Truth, and the Way of Seeming ('seeming' is also translated as 'belief' and 'opinion')." It practically sounds like the Liar Riddle.

That's worth a double take. Parmenides's poem could be the first account of the genesis of dualism in the West. And it is a fair question if it precedes the writing of Genesis, although it certainly does not precede the oral tradition. Maybe it's not a smoking gun, but it is a decent conspiracy theory.

One contrast that I will draw out for the reader is that in the Way of Truth, something either is or isn't. That seems to gel with basic binary thinking. It is Heraclitus who will say both it is and is not the same thing.

Admittedly, some of his poem is abstruse and cryptic. But some of it is unmistakable genius. Before 500 BC Parmenides is laying down a theory of atoms, and using dialectic to do it.

Just like the parables of Jesus, interpreters of Parmenides have wanted to derive a "moral of the story." What does it mean? I think Plato has probably set the tone here. In Plato's Church of Reason, Parmenides is the author of the genesis of dualism. And the dogma is that truth is One. And Plato's friends are allowed into the truth, and Plato's enemies are not. And every group of elitists, people that think they can and should make decisions for other people, are denominational descendants of Plato's Church of Reason. Every single one.

But in some places Parmenides and Heraclitus sound the same. They both say that the cosmos is eternal. Heraclitus just says it's like an eternally changing fire. There is a Way of Truth and a Way of Seeming. But nondualism can't just knee jerk against dualism without breaking its own nature.

I will write it like one of the chiasms of Heraclitus: it is both Heraclitus and Parmenides, Parmenides and Heraclitus.

And it isn't.

74

Was Jesus forsaken on the cross?

This is something the chaplain better think about. This is something you need to know. This is on the test. A lot of people feel forsaken. And when they do, if they have been taught that they will never be forsaken, something in their spirit breaks and sometimes forever.

This is an important doctrinal question. With the trinitarian structure, it is said that Father and Son can never be separated. Dogmatically, the answer has to be no.

But that's not the end of the story or question. "Never leave nor forsake" is an important phrase. It occurs in the Torah, in the prophets (although there in concept), in Chronicles, and in the Letter to the Hebrews. If you wanted to find a thread that tied together the Moses tradition, the

David tradition, and the New Testament, this is a good thread. And, if Jesus is officially forsaken, it's a terrible thread.

But seriously, if Jesus wasn't forsaken on the cross, who was? What does it take to get forsaken? If it doesn't apply to Jesus, to whom does it? Brutalized, strung up, and naked. It is the most famous state-sponsored execution in all history, recorded or not.

Moreover, the man himself said so. That should count for something. He says, "My God, my God, why hast thou forsaken me?" If the man who has to suffer and die identifies himself as forsaken, doesn't that qualify as forsaken? When Jesus says, "I am the Way," dogmatically that is held to be true. Why is it any less doctrinal, any less so, when he says, "My God, my God, why hast thou forsaken me?"

What is utterly fascinating here is precisely how he laments. He could lament against the tradition itself. Like Job's friends and wife advise him, "Job, you are done, clearly your life is behind you, just curse God and die." Such would be for Jesus to lament outside the tradition. But Jesus is lamenting from *within* the tradition. He is quoting Psalm 22. Word for word.

> My God, my God, why hast thou forsaken me? why art thou so far from helping me, and from the words of my roaring? O my God, I cry in the daytime, but thou hearest not; and in the night season, and am not silent. But thou art holy, O thou that inhabitest the praises of Israel. Our fathers trusted in thee: they trusted, and thou didst deliver them. They cried unto thee, and were delivered: they trusted in thee, and were not confounded. But I am a worm, and no man; a reproach of men, and despised of the people. All they that see me laugh me to scorn: they shoot out the lip, they shake the head, saying, "He trusted on the LORD that he would deliver him: let him deliver him, seeing he delighted in him." But thou art he that took me out of the womb: thou didst make me hope when I was upon my mother's breasts. I was cast upon thee from the womb: thou art my God from my mother's belly. Be not far from me; for trouble is near; for there is none to help. Many bulls have compassed me: strong bulls of Bashan have beset me round. They gaped upon me with their mouths, as a ravening and a roaring lion. I am poured out like water, and all my bones are out of joint: my heart is like wax; it is melted in the midst of my bowels. My strength is dried up like a potsherd; and my tongue cleaveth to my jaws; and thou hast brought me into the dust of death. For dogs have compassed me: the assembly of the wicked have inclosed me: they pierced my hands and my feet. I may tell all my bones: they look and stare upon me. They part my garments among them, and cast lots upon my vesture. But be

not thou far from me, O LORD: O my strength, haste thee to help me. Deliver my soul from the sword; my darling from the power of the dog. Save me from the lion's mouth: for thou hast heard me from the horns of the unicorns.

For a moment my eye is drawn to the line, "I am poured out like water." Over two thousand years, you forget how messy this is. Over two thousand years, you forget what it means to be visceral and embodied. Yes, one forgets the viscera of life. Paul will latch onto these words in the theory of *Kenosis*, a central self-emptying in the work of midwifery.

Even in this moment when someone would feel completely abandoned by God, completely severed from anything resembling God's plan, Jesus is saying, "Even this agony is part of a greater story, and it has always been so." Critics say that the similarity of Jesus on the cross to this psalm is the result of writers trying to make it look prophetic, trying to force the prophecy to work out. These scholars actually use this textual similarity as an argument that Jesus categorically *didn't* say these things.

But what if this was something else? What if something else is going on here? What if this is a man who is dying, and he gets the last word on what his execution means? That is, what if Jesus is defining the meaning of his death by using Scripture? What if this is his own alchemy and transmutation? This would change everything. What if "being forsaken" actually means "being engrafted—forever"? I don't think I'm going to come up with anything this inspired to say when I die. To me, these words, and that these words are the quotation of a tradition, and that these words that simultaneously confirm and contradict that tradition, are more transcendent than the resurrection itself.

And this is precisely why chaplaincy is so important. It is not just where we get to tell our own story on our own terms and exercise our autonomy, although that happens. It is also the place, and maybe the only place, where we get to decide what story holds our story. This is the sacrament of life review. This is why we must collect those unwritten novels. Because that is where we claim the greater story, and it claims us.

So, that settles it. Jesus was, and was not, forsaken. This is the culmination of something I once named "Resurrection Logic." This is called: "Quantum Christianity."

Chapter 19

The Desert

> Abstraction today is no longer that of the map,
> the double, the mirror or the concept.
> Simulation is no longer that of a territory,
> a referential being or a substance.
> It is the generation by models of a real without origin or reality:
> a hyperreal.
> The territory no longer precedes the map, nor survives it.
> Henceforth, it is the map that precedes the territory
> —precession of simulacra—
> it is the map that engenders the territory
> and if we were to revive the fable today,
> it would be the territory whose shreds are slowly rotting across the map.
> It is the real, and not the map, whose vestiges subsist here and there,
> in the deserts which are no longer those of the Empire, but our own.
> The desert of the real itself.
>
> BAUDRILLARD

75

There are no secrets in the desert.

How can you have a secret if there is no one to keep it from?

Round the turn with me. Let us think about the desert, manna, and secrets once more.

I long for the desert. Let us think again about secrets and lies. Because every lie is a secret, but not every secret is a lie. This where the chiasm meets chasm. It is in the desert where we meet God, from whom no secret is hid, even as Jesus urges us to pray in secret. Jesus is not saying: pray in secret; rather, pray in desert.

You do wind up carrying things. This is inevitable. Even if you don't meet anyone, there is still the conversation in your head. You see things, you think about things. Some of its going to stick.

You begin to believe that the problem is that no one knows what you are carrying. That for some reason, you are hiding it. You never decided to hide it, but the solitude generates a *de facto* sense of secrecy, because no one knows.

At first, you don't even see this happening because the desert is fraught with survival and pressing concerns.

As the days move on, you reach a point where you become completely incommunicable and untranslatable. Your perspective has evolved into something truly different. The experience feels a little bit like *I Am Legend*, that overnight the human race has disappeared, that you are the only one left who experiences the human condition: the frightening thought that humanity has shifted under your feet.

That's not exactly right. Perhaps you could write the perfect description that would allow another to understand your experience. Perhaps you could find an oasis, and shelter, and write everything down.

But if you could, it doesn't really matter. If you stay at the oasis, you die at the oasis. You cannot cross the desert this way.

Moving further into the desert demands everything. All of the attention. And all of the focus. Being understood by another is revealed as the luxury that it is. The desert has you. Having that shared perspective does nothing to change what it means to cross the desert.

But you can let go of all those things you are carrying. You can travel lightly.

There are no secrets. You have not killed someone like Cain (the renegade for whom the gig is up), and run off in eternal shame. You are crossing the desert. The things you see are hard to describe. There are not many for whom to describe them.

But you are open. Unencumbered. You can come out of your prayer closet, and be honest, and still pray in privacy. Outdoor prayer is the gift of the desert.

There are no secrets but there are confidences and considerations. This is the complicated reality of things. There are very few people who have one name, all the time. We grant this royalty to celebrities, Bono, Cher, and other people of one name, and we admire them for it. We say they are authentic because they get to exude the same noxious behavior everywhere. This is extremely privileged to the point of being infantilized. Most of us, without power or branding, have to navigate very complicated social circles like everyone else. We modify accordingly.

Like Kaufman says, we crave simplicity. We get entitled. We convince ourselves that we deserve simple. We should express all of our opinions everywhere always and we deserve to be loved for it. This is what passes for authentic. This is like a baby who brandishes the same dirty diaper everywhere, except that it's not cute. But we publish our philosophical platforms for all to see. If one position is out of alignment with the party, we are demonized as inauthentic and canceled forthwith. In this context, "authentic" means "how good of a dualist you are."

"Integrity" becomes perverted. "Integrity" means "can you hold together this peculiar prescription of predefined positions that are otherwise untenable." If I want you to accept a different idea—even an opposite idea—all I have to do is cram it into the crowded platform, and if you don't everyone you imagine that you are connected to will cancel you.

There are stories that are not mine to tell and it gets complicated.

I will release another truth about myself. I have not had a "call."

There has not been one burning bush. There has not been one defining event. There has not been one moment, not even a day, or a week, where I could tell the singular story: this was how I was called by God.

No, I have not had a call. There has only been a constant calling. There is a funny thing in the text. Believers often refer to the "still small voice of God." In Hebrew we learned that "Qol" is voice or thunder. *Kol d'mama daka*. To translate it would be the "thunder of nothingness." Perhaps the Hebrew would be, "the voice of a thin silence." This is Simon and Garfunkel's "Sound of Silence."

Like Kafka's trumpet, this urge rises within me and I try. Typically, when I start the day, my body hurts. My body does not enjoy the rediscovery of gravity. The sand burns, I suppose. They say the remedy for burning sand is to keep moving. This keeps your foot off the sand as much as on it.

We stagger through the human condition, confused by the forces and indignities thrust upon us. There is daily bread, even if the bread be thin or bare. It is a form of survivalism, I know that. That never sounds very good, "Oh, I'm surviving . . ." Those people are often living in a constant state of trauma. What I'm trying to describe is surviving without the tone of trauma. The ruggedness of Anacharsis comes to mind: "My clothing is a Scythian cloak, my shoes are the hard soles of my feet, my bed is the earth, my food is only seasoned by hunger—and I eat nothing but milk and cheese and meat. Come and visit me, and you will find me at peace." We usually think of flourishing as intrinsically abundant, but in the desert things flourish carefully. There's not a lot, but what I have is where I need it, wherever I may roam.

76

I remain curious about many things. I am curious about the Great Mother.

Lao Tzu writes about the Great Mother. Chapter 20 is especially powerful. I quote it when I talk about negation and midwifery. Today I look at the whole chapter, and I see a manifesto of nondualism. He starts by calling out good and evil in the first few lines, in what could be a reference to Heraclitus or Parmenides, Genesis, or all of the above.

> Give up learning, and put an end to your troubles.
> Is there a difference between yes and no?
> Is there a difference between good and evil?
> Must I fear what others fear? What nonsense!
> Other people are contented, enjoying the sacrificial feast of the ox.
> In spring some go to the park, and climb the terrace,
> But I alone am drifting, not knowing where I am.
> Like a newborn babe before it learns to smile,
> I am alone, without a place to go.
> Others have more than they need, but I alone have nothing.
> I am a fool. Oh, yes! I am confused.
> Others are clear and bright,
> But I alone am dim and weak.
> Others are sharp and clever,
> But I alone am dull and stupid.
> Oh, I drift like the waves of the sea,
> Without direction, like the restless wind.
> Everyone else is busy,
> But I alone am aimless and depressed.
> I am different.
> I am nourished by the great mother.

Lao Tzu also talks about the "Mother of 10,000 things" and of course I also wonder if that is the Great Mother. We say it as a cliché: "Necessity is the mother of invention." Changing the words slightly it sounds less Ben Franklin. "Hunger gives birth to creativity." Or more dryly, "Nature is a mother."

I want to know everything. I am intrigued by what is written and I am intrigued by what is not written. As a fairly traditional Christian, I've always enjoyed that the *Tao* makes no claims about the Godhead. It is like a religious building with no images in that regard, and so, I may enter. However, "Great Mother" is an engendered term. It begs for an antiphonal "Great Father." And there is no "Great Father" here or anywhere. There is a Trinity, though. Lao Tzu mentions that which cannot be named, that which can, and a great Source of them both. This is a variation of Buber's twofold attitude, which hovers as a great Transcendence shimmering over the cataphatic (named) and the apophatic (unnamed). It is mesmerizing that Buber's and Lao Tzu's cosmological nondualisms rest in relationship, dialogue, and names of address.

I want to know what Lao Tzu meant. But even more, I want to know who he read. We read him as ancient, but he references his own sages and ancients. Who were they? Could it be the Seven Sages of Antiquity? What he describes here in this chapter sounds like the milk of Anacharsis. It's certainly possible, now that we know Heraclitus and Lao Tzu have Cyrus-Darius in common.

I wonder how well Heraclitus knew Lao Tzu. I wonder what mother he found in the Temple of Artemis where he placed his philosophy and where he took refuge. I have long thought that there has been a powerful lineage between Heraclitus and Socrates, and that this heritage has been all but blotted out by the apostate Plato. Artemis is the goddess of midwives, and that's a name Socrates takes up as his own. I am very interested in the Artemis tradition. It is Heraclitus himself that imbues the Artemis tradition with the legacy of *Logos*. The *logos* itself may be the only way to transcend beyond this infernal engenderment. Indeed, after examining millennia of philosophy and spirituality that is the most exhausting ennui of all: the genitals.

Of course, the best way to hide something is to bury it with idolatry. All you have to do is sully the Great Mother with idolatry and the stage is set to revert to centuries of male solar worship. I don't think the Artemis tradition an absolute truth, but within its context it is a very compelling pushback against the masculine dualism of Cyrus-Darius. I don't agree with the Reformed theology of Calvin, but even that makes sense within its context against the selling of indulgences.

But we can go older than Heraclitus. Solomon was around five hundred years before Lao Tzu. We think that the book of Proverbs, the wisdom of Solomon, was written at least by 700 BC. This is plenty of time to fertilize the imagination of Heraclitus and Lao Tzu. In Proverbs 8, the feminine spirit of wisdom is speaking:

> The fear of the LORD is to hate evil: pride, and arrogancy, and the evil way, and the forward mouth, do I hate. Counsel is mine, and sound wisdom: I am understanding; I have strength. By me kings reign, and princes decree justice. By me princes rule, and nobles, even all the judges of the earth. I love them that love me; and those that seek me early shall find me. Riches and honour are with me; yea, durable riches and righteousness. My fruit is better than gold, yea, than fine gold; and my revenue than choice silver. I lead in the way of righteousness, in the midst of the paths of judgment: That I may cause those that love me to inherit substance; and I will fill their treasures. The LORD possessed me in the beginning of his way, before his works of old. I was set up from everlasting, from the beginning, or ever the earth was. When there were no depths, I was brought forth; when there were no fountains abounding with water. Before the mountains were settled, before the hills was I brought forth: While as yet he had not made the earth, nor the fields, nor the highest part of the dust of the world. When he prepared the heavens, I was there: when he set a compass upon the face of the depth: When he established the clouds above: when he strengthened the fountains of the deep: When he gave to the sea his decree, that the waters should not pass his commandment: when he appointed the foundations of the earth: Then I was by him, as one brought up with him: and I was daily his delight, rejoicing always before him . . .

I'll ask it straight out: is Solomon giving voice to the "Great Mother"? If there's anything eternal about the Artemis tradition it is only that within which resonates with this, here.

This begets an important resonance to thought in Kaballah: the *tzimtzum*. If God is an infinite Being, and wishes to create life that is truly distinct and free, there has to be some space to put it. If God takes up all the room, being infinite, where is there any room for reality as we know it? Therefore, it is conjectured that there is a Divine contracture, the *tzimtzum*, where the Being of God recedes like waters to make room for creation. Once the emptiness, or void, has been created, there is room for the cosmos and Adam and Eve and the rest of it. The great void where we find our reality is like a cosmic uterus, a celestial matrix.

77

I get into debates. What is the purpose of the Law? Why does God make rules? Is the purpose of the Law, ultimately, compliance? There is another question which I recognize, which I want to set aside, and that is: why did God give the Law to the Jews? Also a good question, but most people who believe in God, Jews and non-Jews, take the Law, "Thou shall not kill," as binding and in effect.

I cannot think that it is; I cannot think that the purpose of the Law is compliance. For one, there are plenty of things in the universe that just are, like the speed of light or gravity itself. It would seem that if God wanted the universe to operate one way and no other, then that would be how the world is instead of making it contingent on successful compliance.

Moreover, the rate of compliance has been abysmal. Tradition holds that Adam got it wrong on day one. If God is a divine Compliance Officer, things are not going very well. Like a failing corporation that keeps score, "It has been three days since an employee fatality," it has been about half a second since God's law was violated; that is, if transgression itself is never-ending and we can clearly mark the end of one sin and the beginning of the next. With eight billion of us mucking around, and the fact that it's always five o'clock somewhere, we can see why we can't keep a running tally.

If God creates reality and humanity, and God creates the Law, you can ask a very similar question about humanity itself. What is the purpose of humanity? Is the purpose of humanity, ultimately, compliance? Is the image of God such a vivid reflection that the reflection is only reflexive? Are we as dumb and unimportant as the mirror? Are we just to be here to travel through the cosmos at our designated sub-light speed?

Or is there something more?

This is where I come back to Radical Monotheism. What if God doesn't want dominance over every living thing? What if what God actually seeks is relationship? The psalm says, "Seek ye first the kingdom of God," but what if in all actuality, the kingdom of God has been seeking you? With that perspective, the Law is more a survival guide to life in the desert. Such a Law is more of a love letter. The very first command is not to put other gods before God. Radical Monotheism, and this applies to the idol of dualism. The words of Wisdom here reverberate through my whole being. "I love them that love me; and those that seek me early shall find me." Could it be? It is one thing to love Wisdom, but what if she promises to love you back? Is this what Pythagoras meant so long ago at the very beginning of philosophy, this love of Sophia?

For a moment, it may be lost on the reader why there is anything radical about monotheism, especially when reading a book by an ordained Christian author. Why should it be radical at all to say that Divinity is One and Unity and not the entire manifold reality of multiplicity? Because it is radical to seriously say that there is One Divine Consciousness that is Creator.

If you were all-powerful, how would you explore relationship? If you were filthy rich, how would you find a relationship with someone who loved you for you? Would you go on a dating app? Would you go on social media and tell the world of how much you had to offer? Or would you hide, hide your power and wealth? Is this the archetype of the prince disguised as a pauper?

Could it be that the possibility of love has brought you here—not even love, but the possibility of love? That you are here exactly because God is trying to have a relationship with you? Because the succulent only blooms in the desert?

CHAPTER 20

The Apocalypse

> Now,
> with God's help,
> I shall become myself.
>
> KIERKEGAARD

78

It was 2019. *Frozen 2* came out on a birthday and we went. I loved the music. How do we follow the Divine Spirit? How do we leave everything we have known? How do we step into our power? How do we become ourselves? These are the greatest questions.

The next year would have some very gruesome ways of answering them. It is hard to relay what happened next. In part, because we were all there. This is why the trial of Socrates is given the weight and credence of more historical accuracy: the jury was five hundred men.

Each of us lost too much in the pandemic. There were little things and loved ones. There was no one that was not touched; even children stopped going to school. Soon, the small losses were deeply tied to a sense of losing everything and the end of the world. The CDC tells us that the answer is hand sanitizer, and there are shortages. And the personal stories are still too vivid. People struggled to breathe and families struggled to grieve. They could not say goodbye to the sick.

The hospital chaplain had a strange piece of this, which doesn't mean much because everything was strange. Suddenly our churches (meaning the hospital itself, although this was also true for churches) were no longer safe to enter, and not just dangerous to ourselves, but to everyone we love and live with. There was this early period of time where there were no tests, there were no vaccines, there were asymptomatic carriers, and there were no proven and trusted methods of treatment. There are details that cannot be told, both hallowed and horrific. A strange detail is that by April, I develop a cough. It is not COVID, but it never goes away.

This is how the Center of Pastoral Care came to a close. The different components that were tied together came apart. The widening gyre could not hold. The first piece that came off was the long-term care facility and nursing home. What the Center for Pastoral Care did was teaching how to do chaplaincy visits. Very quickly there were no visits at all. The second piece was the psychiatric hospital. With demands increasing at my medical hospital, which was my full-time job, I walked away from the private psychiatric center.

The summer got worse. On May 25, George Floyd is murdered. The world watches in slow and helpless horror. We lash out in unfocused anger. More violence, more death, more racism.

By the end of June, both my parents will have COVID. I cannot go. They are in Florida, they quarantine. By August, my father will die. He does not die directly from oxygen deprivation. From the neurological effects of the disease, he loses the ability to swallow. He loses nutrition. He will never be strong enough to overcome the underlying COVID. They are reluctant to place a feeding tube, in part because he continues to test positive. But in the end he chooses not to. He wants to go home, but he dies in the hospital on the day of his discharge.

At the same time, decisions are made to close the Center for Pastoral Care. December 31 will be my last day. I started there the week of 9/11. It is a strange tenure, bookended by national disaster. Odd that it's only nineteen years. Even still, I manage to work through Hanukkah and Christmas and the end of the year. There is, at least, enough oil in the lamps for that.

I am thankful.

I am being moved. I am being uprooted from one pot to the next. My context is being changed for me and without me. And although the hand of God is everywhere it is more intense than I can stand.

79

As I teach chaplaincy, one of the concepts I come back to is that "the meaning of things is revealed in death." For all of my coinage, I cannot claim that. These are the kinds of words that you hear and cannot forget. They stay with you until they make sense of themselves. But I cannot remember where I heard them or find any source attribution. They echo in the voice of Frederick Buechner, but I can't find them anywhere but my own heart.

The words are true in many ways. Someone dies and people come to the funeral that never knew each other. Things come to light. Connections and relationships are revealed. Even siblings can find each other for the first time, believe it or not. The corners and recesses of our heart where the deceased once was are now shown to be empty. This is grief.

This is also what the word *apocalypse* means in Greek. This is what it means when the truth is "unveiled." Following the death of my father, I struggle to hold on. At times, my grip slips.

In my last letters to my father, I share with him Psalm 139. He was discouraged. I did not know it at the time, but the psalm had been very important to him as a young man. I'll reproduce a few words here:

> Whither shall I go from thy spirit? or whither shall I flee from thy presence? If I ascend up into heaven, thou art there: if I make my bed in hell, behold, thou art there. If I take the wings of the morning, and dwell in the uttermost parts of the sea; Even there shall thy hand lead me, and thy right hand shall hold me. If I say, Surely the darkness shall cover me; even the night shall be light about me. Yea, the darkness hideth not from thee; but the night shineth as the day: the darkness and the light are both alike to thee. For thou hast possessed my reins: thou hast covered me in my mother's womb.

This is the sound of Radical Monotheism. God is everywhere. Where can we go to get away from God? Neither heaven nor hell. From God's perspective, the great antinomies of life are overcome; day and night look the same, dualism no more. I hold tightly to this psalm in my grief. I am frightened.

I look everywhere. I return to the ancient Christian document. The *Didache*. The first two verses: "There are two ways, one of life and one of death! and there is a great difference between the two ways. The way of life is this: First, you shall love God who made you. And second, love your neighbor as yourself, and do not do to another what you would not want done to you." This is the Shema all over again. This is two roads and the yellow wood. This is overcoming the Tree of Dualism. *This is Radical Monotheism.*

In trying to overcome my own dualism, I find the words of mystic philosopher Martin Buber to be helpful. For the record, thus has been the purpose of the entire project: to work out my own dualism with fear and trembling. I do not like to take small quotes from him. One feels shamefully irreverent for interrupting a great thinker and a beautiful man. This is from his masterpiece about "I and Thou," and the great dialogue in between.

> The You-sense of the man who in his relationships to all individual Yous experiences the disappointment of the change into It, aspires beyond all of them and yet not all the way toward his eternal You. Not the way one seeks something: in truth, there is no God-seeking because there is nothing where one could not find him. How foolish and hopeless must one be to leave one's way of life to seek God: even if one gained all the wisdom of solitude and all the power of concentration, one would miss him. It is rather as if a man went his way and merely wished that it might be *the* way; his aspiration finds expression in the strength of his wish. Every encounter is a way station that grants him a view of fulfillment; in each he thus fails to share, and yet also does share, in the one because he is ready. Ready, not seeking, he goes his way; this gives him the serenity toward all things and the touch that helps them. But once he has found, his heart does not turn away from them although he now encounters everything in the one. He blesses all the cells that have sheltered him as well as all those where he will still put up. For this finding is not an end of the way but only its eternal center.

Many times, I have thought that the impossible would be possible if I could only hear God whisper, "I love you." That would have been miracle enough on my darkest days. Buber here is more hopeful, suggesting that the path back to God is the path already with God. It is to find oneself along another road, the road to Emmaus. And, maybe, that self-actualization is a legitimate means of exploring, or at least engaging, the Divine. To embrace what one was created to be is to honor the Creator.

80

By the strangest turn of events, I am forced to concede the fact that I am loved. Help flows in. From neighbors, from strangers, from above. I have new friends, people I have never known start caring about me. And, I need them. And my needs are met.

My model is wrong. I don't have three friends; I have many. I have my friend in Oregon, and my friend in Ocracoke. Several good friends in Carolina, Durham and Davidson. And more. I can no longer console myself with the perverse fantasy that I am unloved. I struggle to receive the help for a dozen reasons. Yes, life remains intense; yes, I am not used to it; yes, I am grieving; yes, it reverses my peculiar narrative; yes, there are questions about which I remain uncertain; yes, it is humbling (although not new, but on top of everything it's too much). Communities and groups have been unkind to me in formative ways, but this is something different. I learn it.

I reevaluate everything.

Dualism is an exploitation of the fact that we were created, in order to create polarization. Like the earth itself, dualism is a magnet and a magnet is dualism. I am interested to explore magnetic field theory, and bring that back into my awareness of dualism. Like I said, I'm only a chaplain and I have to pick up a lot along the way. But I ask questions. Is dualism only a spiritual magnet, to attract us to something other than God? Magnets aren't a thing, not like we are used to conceiving. They are not isolated elements. A pound of gold is a pound of gold, all the way through. Magnets are systems of dynamic relationships. A piece of a magnet is an entire magnet, because it's a system. Break one in half and you won't have a positive half and a negative half, but two whole magnets. A magnet is actually a system, and it can be as small as the souvenir on your fridge or as large as the entire planet. It is, essentially, a polarized fractal.

81

For pages, I have tried to be open because for months I hide what I think. Each word disrobes another truth. Can I lift this veil for you? Can I bare this? Will you see me? I am so tired of holding back. I tire of the endless edit. My experience is that I think a lot, and that might be simply because nothing else works as well. Nothing else is easy or effortless. My thoughts are what I have to give. May I share this part of myself with you?

How are we to wander this earth? Are we Cain or Moses? Are we Ishmael or Israel? Are we exiled into the desert, or is the desert a path to somewhere? And just maybe that somewhere is the only place that was ever worth going.

I have learned a few things. There are some things, ahead, that are going to be more intense than I could want. Most people would call this "intensity" "extreme" or "painful." Many people call this "suffering." This is unavoidable and perhaps the greatest suffering is to think otherwise; that it is avoidable.

Even in such intensity, God is there. Holding onto that is essential for this way of nondualism. This, I think, is sonship. Until you can get on the other side of suffering the dualism will tug at you. The point of this is not to consecrate abuse or suffering. The point is to transubstantiate it.

This word *sonship* has always been difficult for me, to some extent because it is engendered but to a much greater degree because I was adopted.

I have resisted various forms of the prosperity gospel, which says we know God's love through our affluence, and achieving the fullness of this blessing requires proclaiming your privilege. But if the sonship of Christ still leads through Psalm 22, then I too can say, "Our Father."

Sonship is a problem. We argue, if there is a God, and if God loves me, God won't create me to suffer. We start from here, and we bend and twist, bend and twist. Before long, we are convinced that if there is a God it is God's obligation to give us what we want. Of course, we would never say it so brazenly and brashly, but that is the crux of it. "Maybe," we backpedal ashamed by our undeniable hubris, "we don't get everything we want, we don't need to be rich (as if that's too sinful so we pretend to not want that), but that God would at least spare us from the really, really bad stuff." The child wants the eternal Parent to be fair. The adolescent wants the reward and punishment system to be transparent. But this is only a means of manipulating God. The adolescent follows the Law, because God would thus be bound by the reward and punishment system. "I ate my broccoli," he says defiantly. "You owe me my ice cream." The word "owe" is pronounced with such stifled rage that it is dripping with disdain.

Really? That's how this goes? God owes you? Were you there? Really? Were you at the creation of the heavens and the earth? Did you tumble with Leviathan?

If we got what we wanted from God, the human condition would not be recognizable, and not for the better. For this, Heraclitus says, "It is not good for men to get all that they want." If bad things only happened to bad people, that would be sheer totalitarian terror. If you think we are afraid of wrath now, imagine if bad things only happened to bad people—how long could you live under such tyranny? We would never figure out who we are. We would never figure out which flavor or fashion we like: we would only fret over what was right, wrong, and wrath. Here's the deal: "You did nothing, and you created nothing. You will receive many blessings. They are all on loan, and you will let go of all of them." Adults understand this. In the meantime we are permitted a few questions. What kind of person do you want to become? In Buber's phrase, "What kind of attitude do you want to have?" What kinds of relationships do you want to have? What do you want to do with God? Anything?

Today, Isaiah finds me: "When thou passest through the waters, I will be with thee; and through the rivers, they shall not overflow thee: when thou walkest through the fire, thou shalt not be burned; neither shall the flame kindle upon thee." Whether or not I can cross it twice, old Heraclitus, I can cross it with God and that is what I need.

At the end of it all, I ask myself what will I adopt as my own? Heraclitus gets at this by saying, "We should not act like the children of our parents." He means, "Grow up." The point of life is not so that we forever imagine ourselves as our parents' children, perpetually becoming older children. The idea is that this eternal adolescent defiance is not a good look.

Freud says, "A boy does not become a man until he buries his father." My father is dead from COVID. I see him for the last time on a computer screen in my office. I rebuild. I start a business, which for now offers CPE, the Institute for Spiritual Midwifery. Even this will not last forever.

It is time for me to take another circuit. It is time for me to find the labyrinth again. It is time for me to return as wayfarer. Another turn, another mile, another turn, another mile. I am—and I am not—coming back. I strain my deafness towards Buber once more.

> But the path is not a circle. It is the way. Doom becomes more oppressive in every new eon, and the return more explosive. And the theophany comes ever *closer*, it comes ever closer to the sphere *between beings*—comes closer to the realm that hides in our midst, in the between. History is a mysterious approach to closeness. Every spiral of its path leads us into deeper corruption and at the same time into more fundamental return. But the God-side of the event whose world-side is called return is called redemption.

I have not had the kind of mystical insight or experience that produces a book like *I and Thou*. Back from my seminary days, and my journaling then, I had found the words, "I, sinner, repent." Sinner is an appositive here; this is not a list of three words. For the longest time, it was only "I, sinner." These words were meant to pattern a series of spiritual movements. The first two words represent the transformation from consciousness to awareness. The last two words were meant to represent the movement from awareness to decision. I felt compelled to write those words, but those were the only two movements that I could identify, as first and second. Perhaps if there are movements that follow, they rely on God. There are only so many steps of the dance you can do by yourself.

Today I am interested in the word *repent*. I think this is a Christian expression of what Buber means by "return," and perhaps what happens on Yom Kippur and the task of atonement. It reminds me of the *Tao Te Ching*, especially chapter 16, which reads like a guide for meditation.

> Empty yourself of everything.
> Let the mind become still.

> The ten thousand things rise and fall while the Self watches their return.
> They grow and flourish and then return to the source.
> Returning to the source is stillness, which is the way of nature.
> The way of nature is unchanging.
> Knowing constancy is insight.
> Not knowing constancy leads to disaster.
> Knowing constancy, the mind is open.
> With an open mind, you will be openhearted.
> Being openhearted, you will act royally.
> Being royal, you will attain the divine.
> Being divine, you will be at one with the Tao.
> Being at one with the Tao is eternal.
> And though the body dies, the Tao will never pass away.

Remember, "Tao" means "way." Repent, return to the Source, be at one, atone.

I walk the line, but what is the line? Is it a tightrope?

No, it is a labyrinth.

Sometimes, around the tight bends of the labyrinth, you do not see where you are going. You cannot imagine that this new direction will ever move toward the center. And sometimes it feels painfully like you are going in the wrong direction. The only grace is that with the labyrinth, there is only forward and back. Lao Tzu, of some odd kinship to Heraclitus says in Chapter 23, "He who loses the way, is lost." Later, in Chapter 53 he will add, "If I have even just a little sense, I will walk on the main road and my only fear will be of straying from it."

The way is that important to the sojourner. To the circuit rider.

I do not want to lose the way. I think of the Psalmist again, "Search me, O God, and know my heart: try me, and know my thoughts: And see if there be any wicked way in me, and lead me in the way everlasting." Again Psalm 139.

It is not simple anymore. It is so simple when you think you understand what the pieces mean. For so long, I have wanted simplicity. Thoreau celebrates the simple at Walden Pond, catching, as it were, two fishes. Lao Tzu talks about quitting writing and going back to the knotting of rope. That all I had to try for was to live well and die well, and with any luck to love well in the interim. Perhaps of all the losses, this is the hardest to grieve: the simple life and the simple death. I thought I knew what these were and what they meant. As if the purpose of life was to take care of your family and not cause too much trouble. I thought the in-between was mine, but once again, the parentheses of life have shifted. I am in something so much bigger, a much, much bigger story and a much greater love.

In this interstice of my life, I find myself; in finding myself, I call out to You and cry, "Father." Iniquity remains unphased and indifferent to the apocalypse; how could the unconscious possibly take note of the unveiling, much less repent? Instructed at every turn and everywhere to be both hungry and full; to abound and to suffer. The journey remains endless; that much holds firm for me. But it is no longer the journey-to; it has become the journey-with. At one point the dream was a simple life, and a simple death; now neither of these are mine alone. The intensity abides; hallelujah.

Recommended Reading

Baudrillard, Jean. *Simulacra and Simulation*. Translated by Sheila Faria Glaser. Ann Arbor: University of Michigan Press, 2004.
Brickhouse, T. C., and N. D. Smith. *The Trial and Execution of Socrates: Sources and Controversies*. New York: Oxford University Press, 2002.
Buber, Martin. *I and Thou*. Translated by Walter Kaufman. New York: Scribner, 1970.
The Cloud of Unknowing: A New Translation. Translated by Carmen Butcher. Boulder, CO: Shambhala, 2009.
Frankl, Victor. *The Doctor and the Soul*. Translated by Richard and Clara Winston. New York: Vintage, 1986.
Geldard, Richard. *Remembering Heraclitus*. Hudson, NY: Lindisfarne, 2000.
Gill-Austern, Brita L. "The Midwife, Storyteller, and Reticent Outlaw." In *Images of Pastoral Care: Classic Readings*, edited by Robert Dykstra, 218–27. St. Louis: Chalice, 2005.
Gonzalez, Francisco J. *Dialectic and Dialogue: Plato's Practice of Philosophical Inquiry*. Evanston, IL: Northwestern University Press, 1998.
Guenther, Margaret. *Holy Listening: The Art of Spiritual Direction*. New York: Paulist, 1992.
Hanson, Karen R. "The Midwife." In *Images of Pastoral Care: Classic Readings*, edited by Robert Dykstra, 249–56. St. Louis: Chalice, 2005.
Heraclitus. *Fragments: The Collected Wisdom of Heraclitus*. Translated by Brooks Haxton. New York: Viking, 2001.
hooks, bell. *Yearning: Race, Gender, and Cultural Politics*. Boston: South End, 1989.
Hyman, Arthur, J. J. Walsh, and T. Williams. *Philosophy in the Middle Ages: The Christian Islamic and Jewish Traditions*. 3rd ed. Indianapolis: Hackett, 2010.
Jaspers, Karl. *Anaximander, Heraclitus, Parmenides, Plotinus, Laotzu, Nagarjuna*. Edited by Hannah Arendt. Translated by Ralph Manheim. New York: Harcourt, 1990.
———. *Socrates, Buddha, Confucius, Jesus*. Edited by Hannah Arendt. Translated by Ralph Manheim. New York: Harcourt, 1990.
Kierkegaard, Søren. *Attack Upon Christendom*. Translated by Walter Lowrie. Princeton: Princeton University Press, 1944.
———. *The Concept of Anxiety*. Translated by Reidar Thomte. Princeton: Princeton University Press, 1980.
———. *The Concept of Irony with Continual Reference to Socrates*. Edited and translated by Howard V. Hong and Edna H. Hong. Princeton: Princeton University Press, 1989.

———. *Concluding Unscientific Postscripts to Philosophical Fragment*. Edited and translated by Howard V. Hong and Edna H. Hong. Princeton: Princeton University Press, 1992.

———. *The Diary of Søren Kierkegaard*. Edited by Peter P. Rohde. New York: Carol Publishing Group, 1993.

———. *Fear and Trembling*. Translated by Alastair Hannay. Harmondsworth: Penguin, 1985.

———. *The Point of View, Etc : Including The Point Of View for My Work as an Author, Two Notes About 'The Individual' and On My Work as an Author*. Translated by Walter Lowrie. New York: Oxford University Press, 1950.

———. *The Sickness Unto Death: A Christian Psychological Exposition For Upbuilding And Awakening*. Edited and translated by Howard V. Hong and Edna H. Hong. Princeton: Princeton University Press, 1980.

———. *Upbuilding Discourses in Various Spirits*. Edited and translated by Howard V. Hong and Edna H. Hong. Princeton: Princeton University Press, 1993.

———. *Works of Love*. Edited and translated by Howard v. Hong and Edna H. Hong. Princeton: Princeton University Press, 1995.

Nietzsche, Friedrich Wilhelm. *Thus Spoke Zarathustra*. United Kingdom: Oxford University Press, 2005.

Pascal, Blaise. *Selections from the Thoughts, Pascal*. Translated and edited by Arthur H. Beattie. Arlington Heights, IL: Harlan Davidson, 1965.

Pirsig, Robert. *Zen and the Art of Motorcycle Maintenance: An Inquiry Into Values*. New York: HarperCollins, 2006.

Plato, *Complete Works*. Edited by John M. Cooper. Associate editor D. S. Hutchinson. Indianapolis: Hackett, 1997.

———. *The Open Society and Its Enemies, Vol. 2 The High Tide of Prophecy: Hegel, Marx, and the Aftermath*. Princeton: Princeton University Press, 1971.

———. *Parmenides and Theaetetus*. Translated by Benjamin Jowett. N.p.: Regnery, 1951.

———. *Phaedrus*. Indianapolis: The Library of Liberal Arts by Bobbs-Merrill, 1956.

Popper, Karl. *The Open Society and Its Enemies, Vol. 1 The Spell of Plato*. Princeton: Princeton University Press, 1971.

Rahn, Otto. *Lucifer's Court: A Heretic's Journey in Search of the Light Bringers*. Rochester, VT: Inner Traditions, 2008.

Rilke, Rainer Maria. *Letters to a Young Poet*. N.p.: Martino Fine, 2011.

Rubenstein, Richard E. *Aristotle's Children: How Christians, Muslims, and Jews Rediscovered Ancient Wisdom and Illuminated the Middle Ages*. New York: Harcourt, 2003.

Thompson, Josiah. *Kierkegaard*. New York: Alfred A. Knopf, 1973.

Thoreau, Henry David. *Walden and Other Writings*. Edited by Joseph Wood Krutch. New York: Bantam, 1981.

Tzu, Lao. *Tao Te Ching*. Vintage Series, translated by Gia-Fu Feng, Jane English, and Jacob Needleman. New York: Vintage, 1989.

Recommended Music

Spotify: https://open.spotify.com/playlist/2XMa98pRNA9k0jwRDANJ7t?si=3c4a2d21aaf042b4.
Or scan this code in the Spotify app:

Cohen, Leonard. "You Want It Darker." Track 1 on *You Want It Darker*. Columbia Records, 2017, digital download. https://music.apple.com/us/album/you-want-it-darker/1154144036?i=1154144442.

Cohen, Leonard. "Steer Your Way." Track 8 on *You Want It Darker*. Columbia Records, 2017, digital download. https://music.apple.com/us/album/steer-your-way/1154144036?i=1154144456.

October Project. "Adam & Eve." Track 4 on *Falling Farther In*. Sony Legacy, 1995, digital download. https://music.apple.com/us/album/adam-eve/283449869?i=283449873.

Bon Jovi. "Wanted Dead Or Alive." Track 5 on *Slippery When Wet*. Mercury Records, 1986, digital download. https://music.apple.com/us/album/wanted-dead-or-alive/1484688048?i=1484688282.

Metallica. "Wherever I May Roam." Track 5 on *Metallica*. Elektra Records, 1991, digital download. https://music.apple.com/us/album/wherever-i-may-roam/579372950?i=579373083.

Big & Rich. "Live This Life." Track 13 on *Horse of a Different Color*. Warner Bros. Nashville, 2004, digital download. https://music.apple.com/us/album/live-this-life/6748725?i=6748811.

Whitesnake. "Here I Go Again (Radio Mix)." Track 6 on *Whitesnake (30th Anniversary Edition)*. Parlophone Records, 1987, digital download. https://music.apple.com/us/album/here-i-go-again-radio-mix/1270802806?i=1270803250.

Cohen, Leonard. "Traveling Light." Track 6 on *You Want It Darker*. Columbia Records, 2017, digital download. https://music.apple.com/us/album/traveling-light/1154144036?i=1154144454.

Harnell, Joe. "The Lonely Man Theme." Track 7 on *The Incredible Hulk: Original Soundtrack Recording*. Five Jays Music, 2022, digital download. https://music.apple.com/us/album/the-lonely-man-theme/1651934893?i=1651936040.

U2. "The Wanderer" (featuring Johnny Cash). Track 10 on *Zooropa*. Island Records, 1993, digital download. https://music.apple.com/us/album/the-wanderer-feat-johnny-cash/1442968012?i=1442968589.

Guns N' Roses. "Estranged." Track 11 on *Use Your Illusion II*. Geffen, 1991, digital download. https://music.apple.com/us/album/estranged/1389971138?i=1389971338.

Kansas, "Carry On My Wayward Son." Track 1 on *Leftoverture*. Kirshner, 1976, digital download. https://music.apple.com/us/album/carry-on-wayward-son/158580313?i=158580367.

Simon, Paul. "Mother and Child Reunion." Track 1 on *Paul Simon*. Columbia Records/Warner Bros., 1972, digital download. https://music.apple.com/us/album/mother-and-child-reunion/380588824?i=380588827.

Queen. "Innuendo." Track 1 on *Innuendo*. Parlophone/Hollywood Records, 1991, digital download. https://music.apple.com/us/album/innuendo/1440806201?i=1440806204.

Cohen, Leonard. "It's Torn." Track 5 on *Thanks for the Dance*. Columbia Records/Legacy Recordings, 2019, digital download. https://music.apple.com/us/album/its-torn/1480060931?i=1480060945.

Deep Purple. "Smoke on the Water." Track 5 on *Machine Head*. Purple Records, 1972, digital download. https://music.apple.com/us/album/smoke-on-the-water-1997-remix/419655190?i=419655244.

Twisted Sister. "We're Not Gonna Take It (2016 Acoustic Recording)." Track 12 on *The Best of the Atlantic Years*. Rhino Entertainment Company, 2016, digital download. https://music.apple.com/us/album/were-not-gonna-take-it-2016-acoustic-recording/1154881001?i=1154881310.

Parr, John. "St. Elmo's Fire." Track 16 on *Letter to America*. John Parr Music, 2011, digital download. https://music.apple.com/us/album/st-elmos-fire-acoustic-live/440725540?i=440725629.

Cohen, Leonard. "Hallelujah." Track 5 on *Various Positions*. Columbia Records, 1983, digital download. https://music.apple.com/us/album/hallelujah/192677178?i=192678693.

October Project. "Falling Farther In." Track 10 on *Falling Farther In*. Sony Legacy, 1995, digital download. https://music.apple.com/us/album/falling-farther-in/283449869?i=283449879.

Edwards, Misty. "You Won't Relent" (featuring David Brymer). Oasis House, 2011, digital download. https://music.apple.com/us/album/you-wont-relent-feat-david-brymer/899630204?i=899630217.

Disturbed. "The Sound of Silence." Track 11 on *Immortalized*. Reprise Records, 2015. https://music.apple.com/us/album/the-sound-of-silence/1006937448?i=1006937459.

Idina Menzel and AURORA. "Into the Unknown." Track 3 on *Frozen II (Original Motion Picture Soundtrack)*. Walt Disney, 2019, digital download. https://music.apple.com/us/album/into-the-unknown/1481414042?i=1481414060.

Idina Menzel and Evan Rachel Wood. "Show Yourself." Track 7 on *Frozen II (Original Motion Picture Soundtrack)*. Walt Disney, 2019, digital download. https://music.apple.com/us/album/into-the-unknown/1481414042?i=1481414060.

Bethel Music and Kristene DiMarco. "It is Well (Live)." Track 2 on *You Make Me Brave: Live at the Civic*. Bethel Music, 2014, digital download. https://music.apple.com/us/album/it-is-well-live/862593658?i=862593692.

The Once. "Coming Back to You." Track 4 on *The Once*. Borealis Recording, 2010, digital download. https://music.apple.com/us/album/coming-back-to-you/410583554?i=410583574.

The Neville Brothers. "Bird on a Wire." Track 6 on *20th Century Masters: The Best of The Neville Brothers (The Millennium Collection)*. A&M Records, 1999, digital download. https://music.apple.com/us/album/bird-on-a-wire/1434893960?i=1434894221.